Opera 30 Guide

D0980258

Hugo von Hofmannsthal, an early portrait by Hans Schlesinger, his brother-in-law (reproduced by courtesy of Octavian von Hofmannsthal)

Preface

This series, published under the auspices of English National Opera and The Royal Opera, aims to prepare audiences to evaluate and enjoy opera performances. Each book contains the complete text, set out in the original language together with a current performing translation. The accompanying essays have been commissioned as general introductions to aspects of interest in each work. As many illustrations and musical examples as possible have been included because the sound and spectacle of opera are clearly central to any sympathetic appreciation of it. We hope that, as companions to the opera should be, they are well-informed, witty and attractive.

The Royal Opera is most grateful to The Baring Foundation for sponsoring this Guide.

Nicholas John
Series Editor

30

Arabella

Richard Strauss

Opera Guide Series Editor: Nicholas John

Published in association with
English National Opera and The Royal Opera
assisted by a generous donation from The Baring Foundation

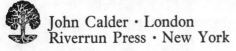

John Calder · London
Riverrun Press · New York

First published in Great Britain, 1985 by
John Calder (Publishers) Ltd.,
18 Brewer Street,
London W1R 4AS

First published in the U.S.A., 1985 by
Riverrun Press Inc.,
1170 Broadway,
New York, NY 10001

BRITISH LIBRARY CATALOGUING IN PUBLICATION DATA
Strauss, Richard
 Arabella. — (Opera guide; 30)
 1. Operas — Librettos
 I. Title   II. Series
 782.1'2   ML50.S/

LIBRARY OF CONGRESS CATALOGING IN PUBLICATION DATA
Strauss, Richard, 1864-1949.
 [Arabella. Libretto. English & German]
 Arabella.

 Opera Guide: 30)
 Libretto by Hugo von Hofmannsthal.
 Discography: p.
 Bibliography: p.
 1. Operas — Librettos.   I. Hofmannsthal, Hugo von.
1874-1929.   II. Title   III. Series
ML50.S918A62 1985   782.1'092'4   82-1822
ISBN 0-7145-4062-5

SUBSIDISED BY THE
Arts Council
OF GREAT BRITAIN

John Calder (Publishers) Ltd, English National Opera and
The Royal Opera House, Covent Garden Ltd receive
financial assistance from the Arts Council of Great Britain.
English National Opera also receives financial assistance from
the Greater London Council.

Typeset in Plantin by Margaret Spooner Typesetting, Dorchester, Dorset
Printed by The Camelot Press, Southampton.

Contents

List of Illustrations

The Edge of the Cliff

Michael Ratcliffe

Arabella is a comedy about fear, panic, social disintegration and love at first sight set on the cliff's edge of Lent. It takes place before, during and after the Viennese Cabbies' Ball on Shrove Tuesday, the last day of Carnival, beyond which there can be no public matchmaking in the ballrooms, no chaperoned and deceptively innocent rides in the Praterhauptallee, no decent pursuit of possible husbands by eligible daughters for six whole weeks. Worse, there will be nothing more on tick. Count Waldner's fifty guilders will hardly see him, his wife and his two highly attractive daughters out into the spring.

From the shuffling and dealing of the cards in the opening bars there is an urgency about the action which affects everybody except Arabella herself, impels her mother Adelaide to the fortune-teller (who, like most fortune-tellers in opera, gets everything right first time), her father to the gaming tables and her younger sister Zdenka to sacrifice Matteo, the man she loves, for the indifferent Arabella whom he adores.

By such a match, Matteo would at least enter the family, financial ruin would be averted and possible — no, certain — sibling complications left to some future date. Zdenka, disguised by the Waldners as a boy because boys are cheaper to run during the Carnival season than girls, is as impulsively neurotic as Chrysothemis in *Elektra*; Arabella warns her not to take the same hysterical and unbalanced road as their mother. For *Arabella* is also a post-Freudian comedy of Vienna in the pre-Freudian age. It is quite clear that, forty years later, Zdenka would have been beating a path to the consulting room at Berggasse, 19, and found the names of her mother and Matteo in the appointment-book before her.

Strauss and Hofmannsthal's final collaboration is an anthology of quintessentially Viennese themes, attitudes and occasions conceived at the end of his life by a poet part Jewish, part Italian, born in 1874 and himself an infant prodigy of the decadent fin-de-siècle, who by turns became classicist, mystic and stoic. Even if Hofmannsthal had not died before Strauss composed a note of the score, we should still see *Arabella* as a farewell piece, a return to the subject and manners of the city explored so richly in *Der Rosenkavalier*.

Both men were at pains to minimise comparisons between their new opera and their greatest success, but even setting aside the matters of inspiration and commitment, some cannot be avoided. The librettist placed *Rosenkavalier* in the Vienna of the early 1740s, when the High Baroque age, glorious in the architecture which may still be enjoyed today, and triumphant in the field, shaded into the more anxious intimacies of Rococo. The greatest anxiety, as well as the deepest source of affection and pride, was that Austria, alone in Europe, was ruled by a woman; it was during these years that the disputed succession of the Empress Maria Theresa provoked Frederick the Great's rape of Silesia — the first of the calamities and disasters, many Austrians believe, to signal the beginning of the end of the Habsburg Empire.

That end, of course, took a dizzying and brilliant century and three-quarters to complete itself, and whilst *Arabella* is placed with simplicity and precision at a particular point on the downward curve ('Place: Vienna. Time: 1860'), it is by no means even the penultimate one. Supposing Arabella and

Viorica Ursuleac, the creator of the title role. Strauss considered her his ideal soprano and she also created the roles of Maria in 'Friedenstag' and the Countess in 'Capriccio' for him (Royal Opera House Archives)

Mandryka get married soon after they complete their reconciliation in the lobby of the modest hotel — and we must hope, before further misunderstandings manifest themselves or the wretched Matteo changes his mind, that they do — they will celebrate their Golden Wedding with the First World War still three or four years away and the Emperor himself good for another six.

The point is that Hofmannsthal's Viennese librettos are both informed by the spirit and the ages in which they are so carefully set: *Rosenkavalier* rests on a climacteric of Viennese history, suffused by a sense of youth, beauty, fulfilment, pride and hope, only briefly darkened by the certainty of impermanence and death; *Arabella* exemplifies an age of materialist energy, speculation, scramble and shock.

The 1860s saw the apotheosis of Johann Strauss in the Volksgarten and at Court, but the waltzes that cut so gorgeous and anachronistic a swathe through *Rosenkavalier* become in *Arabella* the music of slithering, chromatic intrigue and decay which no sooner brings people together than it whirls them apart. These waltzes are a paper currency: they are the music of an inflation which was to ruin so many Viennese speculators on 'Black Friday', in the year before Hofmannsthal himself was born.

Why 1860? Why this milieu? Hofmannsthal told Strauss that his shrewd friends in the theatre had advised him that the period was coming into fashion again and that the public would be ready for it. This is rather typical of Hofmannsthal's supposedly 'commercial' tips, for the *Arabella* correspondence between the two men shows that the composer's theatrical instinct was the finer of the two by this stage, except when he mischievously provoked Hofmannsthal into activity by demanding a 'colossal' Balkan ballet in the second act. Max Reinhardt and the rest were correct as far as European and Hollywood movies were concerned, for the cinema was about to enter the decade of *Camille* and *Gone with the Wind*, but wrong about the theatre, which had to wait until 1951 for *The King and I* to ensure the immortality of the crinoline for certain — and in the opera house, the revival came even later, with Luchino Visconti's meticulously historical production of Verdi's *Traviata* for Maria Callas in 1955.

There is no suggestion in their letters that either Strauss or Hofmannsthal was consciously influenced by the cinema, but *Arabella* is a movie-plot of the time if ever there was one. After the puzzled and/or polite receptions for both *Die Frau Ohne Schatten* (*The Woman Without a Shadow*, 1919), and *Die Aegyptische Helena* (*The Egyptian Helen*, 1928), both men wanted to write a comedy. Anything mythical or heroical', wrote Hofmannsthal, 'makes a modern audience uneasy, anything sombre and grand . . . terrifies them to the marrow of their bones; but give them a hotel lounge, a ballroom, betrothal, officers, cabbies, tradesmen and waiters, and they know where they are.' This proved to be not quite true either, as well as rather patronising, since the hotel lobby (not lounge) in question belongs not to the post-war social comedy of Coward, Stroheim, Molnar or Lubitsch, but to a period about which nobody had thought much for a very long time.

The year Hofmannsthal finally settled on possesses a singular resonance. Viennese history in the mid-nineteenth century is the history of apparently imperturbable calm masking a series of traumatic shocks so deep that in the end they formed the insoluble contusions that led to the First World War. 1860 stands almost exactly half way between the street fighting and fall of Prince Metternich in March 1848 and the spectacular financial collapse of Friday May 9, 1873.

9

Gundula Janowitz as Arabella and Eberhard Wächter as Mandryka at the Vienna State Opera

The 1848 revolution was of such significance that the outwardly innocent Biedermeier years leading up to it are viewed remotely as 'pre-March'. This description (*Vormärz*) may be applied to people as well as to a time: Count and Countess Waldner, who have, one feels, hardly adjusted to the arrival of the 1850s, let alone a decade beyond that, are distinctly *Vormärz* in style: socially maladroit and shabby-genteel, inclined to hoot and puff, they are in danger of being swept away completely in the new city rising around them.

Three years before the opera begins, the Emperor Franz Josef initiated the greatest change to come over Vienna — *his* city, he liked to remind the citizens — since the aristocratic building boom that preceded the events of *Rosenkavalier*. He ordered the razing of the Renaissance city walls and the construction on the former parade-ground dividing the inner city from the suburbs of a great hexagonal boulevard — the Ringstrasse. Along the length of the Ring huge public buildings — the Opera, Stock Exchange, University, Town Hall, Court Theatre, Parliament, concert hall, hotels — alternated with hundreds of private developments to transform the historic *Kaiserstadt* into a *Weltstadt*, outstripping even the Paris which had inspired it because Vienna was not only magnificent but compact.

The resulting mixture is now known as *Historismus*, an eclectic recourse to the past to dignify and adorn the present. The most successful painter of the late Sixties and Seventies was Hans Makart, Rubens of the Ringstrasse, master of imperial ceremonies and illusionist-extraordinary, not quite a fake. All this proceeded with such exuberance and such massive doses of capital investment from abroad that nobody could see as early as 1860 that the transformation of Vienna would herald a false dawn and not a rebirth. It was easy to miss the bandwagon completely, or if you caught it, to get thrown off on the sharp bends because you lacked the means wherewith to hold on. For Vienna, like Count Waldner, was living on credit, and creditors could, from time to time, foreclose. So *Arabella* begins with a stream of unwelcome visitors at the door of the hotel suite.

The distracting beautification of the city was accompanied by disastrous Austrian reverses abroad. Whilst Victorian England was enjoying its years of greatest prosperity and peace after the Crimean War, Austria was defeated in war by Piedmont and the French Emperor in 1859, losing Lombardy and Milan to the emerging Kingdom of Italy, and then Venice and the Veneto after the even more crushing Prussian defeat at Sadowa in 1866. A year later, Austria's current weakness, added to decades of antagonism between the Austrian and Hungarian halves of the empire, produced the constitutional compromise whereby each half became autonomous under The Duel Monarchy of Austria-Hungary. The Viennese called it 'The Empire Under Notice'.

Mandryka's lands would then have been part of the Kingdom of Hungary administered not from Vienna but from Budapest. He would not have been pleased. For Mandryka is from Croatia, and of all the minority ethnic groups in the Habsburg territories by far the loyallest to Vienna were the Croats. That, to Hofmannsthal as well as to Waldner, is doubtless one of the attractions of Herr von Mandryka.

Mandryka represents for the super-aesthete von Hofmannsthal the dream of an effete and ailing cosmopolis renewed in vigour and blood by aan equal partnership with a vigorous Slav south. Most characters in the opera assume that he is from Wallachia, far beyond Hungary towards the Black Sea, but, like all big city people, the Viennese were always a bit vague as to what

11

happened beyond their gates and would quote with malicious approval Metternich's barb that Asia begins at the Landstrasse — about a mile from the present opera house on the north-eastern side. But he may be placed fairly precisely. He speaks in anger of returning home on the next train. He is wealthy, but in order to afford the additional expense of travelling to Vienna along one of the finest railways in Europe, and staying to pay court there, he sells a forest to a Jew living in Sissek — that is, some 35 miles south of Zagreb in present-day Yugoslavia. The hope of the Waldners is that he will bring loyalty, enthusiasm and cash, not rebelliousness, to the old stock. He is a 'Mensch' among pygmies.

Hofmannsthal liked to think of his heroine as, in part, a New Woman whom he compared to Shaw's Saint Joan, but the New Woman vanishes fairly swiftly when the little woman looks up to this big man. Arabella's idyll of a future playing the gracious Balkan chatelaine by Mandryka's side has something very bourgeois about it — her knowledge of husbandry and the peasants is clearly rudimentary — yet there is also something touching about her position as the member of a transient and impoverished family who must fetch the required glass of water from the courtyard of a hotel in a strange city rather than the yard of her own home. (Presumably hotel tap water would not do.)

The economic and psychological health of Vienna in the early Ringstrasse years was highly volatile: total recovery and spectacular disaster succeeded one another with alarming regularity, but whilst the city seems in retrospect to have lurched and waltzed from one smash to the next — there was racing in the Prater and the cafés were full again the day after the news of Sadowa arrived — the building went on. In an earlier draft of *Arabella*, Hofmannsthal had his heroine on the brink of accepting the hand of a building contractor, 'der Richtige' ('the right man') still being out of sight, but the promise of fresh Slav blood took precedence even over new money, and the Balkan imperative won out. Besides, Mandryka is not merely handsome and healthy; he is rich. Strauss objected that Mandryka had no serious competition, and not even the artificial conflicts of the second and third acts, hingeing on one imperfectly overheard remark between the secondary lovers, quite succeeds in meeting the objection.

Hofmannsthal wrote much of the libretto in what he called a 'telegraph', or naturalistic, style. The conversation moves at speed and in great detail, and the pleasures of a performance in the language of the audience are considerable. Throughout, words and music speak of a hectic and nervous society in which the great things of the world are taking place not in the lobby of a small hotel in the inner city where the Waldners cannot pay their bills, but a mile away where new wealth, glamour and power are building the Ring. Hofmannsthal believed that the shell of civilisation was thin and in Vienna, as in all urban cultures, partly depended on intelligence and the use of wealth.

The hindsight of our own and of the librettist's ages tell us that not even Mandryka, the new man, has time on his side. Nothing and nobody except the heroine stands on firm ground in this comedy. Among the neurotic 'telegraph' style of Zdenka and the rest, Arabella's entrance music flows in serenely. She alone has the breadth and strength of mind to see beyond the current crisis, the next excitement, the next bill. She alone will learn the lessons of Shrove Tuesday and practice them for the rest of her life.

Lisa della Casa in the title role at Covent Garden in 1965 (photo: Houston Rogers, Theatre Museum)

Mandryka (Raymond Wolansky) begs Arabella (Heather Harper) to forgive him as Adelaide (Heather Begg) looks on; Covent Garden, 1973 (photo: Donald Southern) and (below) Waldner (Michael Langdon) and Mandryka (Dietrich Fischer-Dieskau) in Act One at Covent Garden, 1965 (photo: Houston Rogers, Theatre Museum)

A Musical Synopsis

William Mann

Hofmannsthal specified several conflicting dates for the incidence of *Arabella*; the final one is 1860, and the action takes place entirely on the morning and evening of Shrove Tuesday of that year. Count Waldner, a retired cavalry officer, lives with his wife and children in a smart hotel in central Vienna. He has exhausted his army pension, and the letterbox is groaning with unpaid bills. His wife Adelaide has grown more superficial, less cultured and less cranky since we first met her as the Widow von Murska in *Lucidor**. Her decision to dress the younger daughter as a boy springs from no tortuous whim but from the severely practical consideration that the parents are too poor to bring out two daughters in Viennese society. Of Arabella's suitors, Matteo (*olim* Vladimir) is no longer her mother's favourite; Adelaide now prefers Count Elemer, one of three rich army playboys who are courting Arabella *en trio*.

Josephine Veasey as Adelaide and Phyllis Cannan as the Fortune Teller, Covent Garden 1981 (photo: Clive Barda)

Silly Countess Waldner is hard at it, when the curtain rises, in consultation with a Fortune-Teller; Strauss, the master of tone-painting, gives a *trompe l'oreille* description of the shuffling and laying out of cards (different from the one in *Intermezzo*; though also used for Count Waldner's card-games). Below the playing-card theme is heard the motif associated with the penniless Waldner family [1, 2]. Zdenka is in the room as well, putting papers in order, perhaps bills, perhaps a new letter that she has written in Arabella's hand to Matteo, assuring him of eternal devotion. Each time the doorbell rings she goes to ward off the creditors.

* for the sources of the libretto, see Patrick J. Smith's article, p. 33.

Sona Ghazarian as Zdenka and Dennis O'Neill as Matteo at Covent Garden in 1981 (photo: Clive Barda)

The Zdenko-Zdenka complex, an odd one at best, makes more sense when one knows the original in *Lucidor*. It might have been made for Strauss to set to music. Strauss had created Octavian and horrified Hofmannsthal by making trouser-roles of the Composer in *Ariadne II* and Dau-ud in *Die Aegyptische Helena* (which he did because he disliked tenors). Now, as if to tease him, Hofmannsthal produced a realistically justified trouser-role.

Adelaide calls to Zdenka to leave the bills on the table; and violas introduce Countess Waldner's own theme [3]. The cards have nothing encouraging to tell her of the legacy that the Waldners expect so anxiously, but they can vividly describe Count Waldner and his ill luck at gambling. Adelaide sets all her hopes on a rich marriage for Arabella, and upper wind match [3] with a rising scale that represents the salvation of the family [4]. Violas launch the career of the merry, charming Arabella theme [5]. The Fortune-Teller has something more helpful to offer on this subject. The Officer whom she sees so clearly, and whom Zdenka identifies as her adored Matteo [6] is not the successful suitor. The bridegroom-to-be is a foreigner, summoned by letter. That he is the Right Man (*Der Richtige*) we know from the Slavonic folk-song quoted briefly by horns [7]. The trumpet identifies him as Mandryka [8]. Adelaide wrongly assumes that he must be Count Elemer, one of Arabella's playboy suitors [9]. She also learns that delay to the successful conclusion of the marriage will come through another girl, Arabella's sister, and Countess Waldner is obliged to explain to the Fortune-Teller about Zdenka [10]. [10a] represents Zdenka's real nature, [10b] her outward appearance as a boy. The Fortune Teller insists that the danger is there; and Adelaide, much embarrassed by the presence of Zdenka, whisks the good lady into her boudoir for a more private session.

Zdenka, left alone, puts the audience further in the picture; Matteo has been forbidden the house by Countess Waldner for fear of compromising other suitors. Zdenka is convinced that Arabella must love him as much as she herself does; she utters a prayer for Matteo and Arabella and money. At the climax, two new themes are introduced. [11] is associated with Zdenka's loving nature. [12] is concerned with Matteo's transports of passionate longing and the little solo ends with a charming slow waltz based on [10a].

Matteo slips quietly into the room [6] for a report on Arabella's activities, and a complaint of her coldness towards him — so opposed to the warmth of her letters. The reason for this is given in a theme played by flute and a moment later by clarinet: this is the opposite of [7]; it means the Wrong Man. Arabella is not, in reality, remotely interested in Matteo [13].

Matteo insists that Arabella must write again this very day, and hurries out with wild threats of foreign service and suicide. Poor Zdenka is at her wits' end when she is fortunately interrupted by Arabella's return from her morning constitutional with a chaperone. Arabella is accompanied by the theme of the Carnival Ball at which she is to be Queen [14].

Today being Carnival Day she has received presents from all her admirers. Her eyes light first on some roses (a half-conscious allusion to the Silver Rose motif) and she asks [4, 8] if a Hussar by any chance brought them for her. In fact they are from Matteo, who is [13]; the entire male sex is divided, for Arabella, into those who are Wrong, and one who will be Right. Arabella puts down the roses hastily, too hastily for Zdenka, who is pained that her adored Matteo should be so scorned by her adored Arabella: the clarinet shows us Arabella through Zdenka's eyes [15].

Arabella turns to the presents from her three noble admirers, whom she

17

The Covent Garden production in 1981: (above) Mandryka (Ingvar Wixell) and Waldner (Manfred Jungwirth) in Act One, and (below, from left to right) Waldner (Manfred Jungwirth), Adelaide (Josephine Veasey), Dominik (Philip Gelling), Lamoral (Roderick Earle), Elemer (Robin Leggate), Mandryka (Ingvar Wixell) and Fiakermilli (Lillian Watson) in Act Two (photos: Clive Barda)

Nan Christie as Zdenka at ENO, 1984 (photo: Clive Barda)

finds excellent company but equally Wrong Men for serious romance ([13] again). Zdenka finds them worthless compared with Matteo, and now [15] on violas and bassoon is mated with a surging arpeggio on the cellos — this is Matteo's third, physically compelling theme [16]. Zdenka pleads Matteo's cause so passionately that Arabella warns her it is time she became a girl at last. I don't want to be a woman like you, cold and a flirt, answers her sister. Arabella is in earnest this time. Strauss slips the gear-lever one notch in the direction of aria as the cor anglais sadly echoes [13], and strings unfold the long melody of Arabella's serious mood [17]. She expounds her continual surprise to find how quickly her heart can warm to a man, and equally quickly turn away from him. And yet she knows that when the Right Man appears [7] she will recognize him at once and never swerve from her love again. This is the famous and sensuously most beautiful duet *Aber der Richtige*.

It is applauded, so to speak, by the jingle of sleighbells in the street. Elemer has won the privilege, over Dominik and Lamoral, of taking Bella for a drive. Because it is Carnival [14] she will go with him, and also because she must make her choice tonight before her coming-out Carnival ends. Zdenka imagines Matteo's suicide if another is chosen [6] — she will find his body, kiss his icy lips. Arabella explains what brought the Hussar into her mind; she saw one, a foreigner, gazing at her in the street this morning, and prayed that he would send her flowers. Mandryka's foreignness is expressed by [18], which is related to [17] (since he and Arabella were made for one another).

Meanwhile here is Elemer, introduced by a Polonaise on [9], and radiant

19

with the triumph of having Arabella to himself, a triumph slightly soured by the necessity of taking her young brother along too. Their conversation (all that is left of the vocal octet in the first version) is jolly and immensely spirited — there is only one pull-up when Arabella talks of having to choose a husband before the night is out. The three Noble Nincompoops, as Strauss neatly described them, exist purely for light and romantic relief. But Elemer is a romantic figure, ardent as well as dashing; the second of his themes makes this clear when the horn softly plays it as he calls her the Queen not only of the Ball tonight but forever [19].

His speech is full of such *fleurettes*, and many of them are answered in the orchestra by [13] or [7]; there is even a classic example of thoughtless label-tying when Strauss brings out the Right Man theme of Arabella's mocking comment that Elemer and his friends are 'a right bunch' (*Ihr seid schon die Rechten*). At one of these gallantries however, about the power of a girl's look, the first violins breathe a theme of longing henceforth much linked with Arabella [20]. As Elemer leaves, she exclaims to Zdenka: her foreigner [18] is outside again. But she dare not hope, for he passes by ([8] sadly, and [4] inverted for 'unsalvation').

Count Waldner comes in, and is met by his wife who dismisses the children — your father has worries, she explains, and [1] tells us why. He scans the letters eagerly; alas they are all bills. He had hoped for a letter from one Mandryka, an old army comrade, rich as Crœsus, a noted womanizer to whom Waldner had sent a portrait of Arabella in the faint hope that the longed-for rich suitor might be he, old man or no. Deaf to Adelaide's proposal that they should all leave Vienna, depressed by the mountain of Final Notices and the absence of even fifty gulden for his luck in the gaming house, Waldner rings for a brandy, only to be told that service in Room 8 must be on a strict cash basis. [8] as well as [1] is in his thoughts, but automatically he dismisses a caller announced by the waiter, then sees a visiting card, and reads the name with joy: Mandryka! The caller is received.

Mandryka is tall, powerfully built and elegant, about thirty-five years of age, his manner is direct and comradely, his appearance fairly suggestive of rusticity (this probably only means that he has a ruddy and cheerful complexion), his behaviour utterly dignified, as his entrance theme ([18] solemnly on horn quartet) and the sombre, rich-toned scoring of the whole scene, full of divided strings and of rests for high-lying instruments all suggests. Waldner goes to meet him with open arms, then recoils in surprise, for this is not his old army comrade. Mandryka explains; he had received a letter from Waldner (it is now bloody, since on the same day he was attacked by a she-bear), passed on to him as the only surviving Mandryka (and therefore [7]) — Waldner's friend, his uncle, being now deceased. He proposes to come at once to the point; Strauss gets there even more quickly with a literally wooing theme, that of Mandryka as suitor [21].

Is the subject of the enclosed portrait, Waldner's daughter, still unbetrothed? Waldner assents. Was the intention that old Mandryka should fall in love with Fräulein Waldner and ask her hand in marriage? Waldner tries to parry this masterpiece of thought-reading. Mandryka, part unfamiliar with Viennese talk, part afraid that some sophisticated urban hint might pass over his head, hangs on Waldner's every embarrassed syllable — and then takes the initiative, using his uncle as an imaginary suitor for Arabella's hand

Opposite: Peter Rice's designs for Covent Garden in 1965 (Royal Opera House Archives)

(a glorious development of [21]). Now that the uncle is dead, he continues, it is the nephew who is the heir to the Mandryka wealth and who himself asks for Arabella to wife; the whole process is carried out with that immensely tactful, longest-way-round-is-the-shortest-way-home verbosity that is indigenous to the countryman. It happens to suit the context by allowing Mandryka a long solo with a rapid *cabaletta* in which he relates the tale of his illness after meeting the bear, the anxiety of his servant, the sale of a forest to get the money to come to Vienna and court Arabella... Quite without boasting Mandryka reveals how enormously rich he is. Gradually the idea of his wealth creeps into the musical texture [22].

And at this point he draws out his wallet to show the proceeds of sale. Waldner stares goggle-eyed at what is no less than an oasis to the thirsty traveller. His enchantment does not pass unnoticed. Mandryka begs to lend him a thousand gulden — as a favour to his prospective son-in-law, he adds tactfully. 'Take some, I mean it!' he offers [23].

Waldner is pressed without embarrassment into accepting two such notes. Mandryka adds that he would wish to meet Arabella and her mother; not now — one must prepare for such a holy occasion — but at some suitable moment — he will be staying in the hotel. And so saying he departs taking with him [17] which is so close to his own [18].

Waldner is almost hysterical with joy at the sudden access of wealth. Again and again he repeats Mandryka's words 'Teschek, bedien' dich!', to the bewilderment of the waiter and Zdenka, and then he leaves in triumph — for the gaming table, of course. Zdenka, (thinking always of Matteo's [12]) is convinced that trouble has softened her father's brain. Matteo makes another brief appearance and is promised a letter at the Ball that night. He escapes as Arabella returns, urging Zdenka to dress for their sleigh ride. For the sleigh ride and, Zdenka adds almost in despair, your Elemer. Zdenka sings the words to the dropping seventh in [20]. At once a solo viola rejects the name with Wrong Man [13], and lower wind and strings admit this is only Zdenka's idea of Arabella's future [15]. It would be sad, says the oboe, if he were the Right Man ([7] in C sharp minor); but the salvation, remarks the viola *en passant*, of the family [4]. This is a typically articulate Strauss orchestral passage. Arabella repeats Zdenka's taunt: 'My Elemer'; it sounds strange. She knows that she longs with overwhelming anxiety for — what? We know the answer to be 'Der Richtige'. He is not [12] Matteo. [7] turns into a quick waltz, but it is still in the minor mode until she thinks again of her handsome, unknown suitor, and then the music comes marvellously to the boil, an inward, restrained boiling-point with strings heavily subdivided as in *Ariadne*. The thought of marriage with Elemer brings out [17] on two soft trombones, as if she were stepping on somebody's grave — is it the foreigner's grave? [7] turns cheerful and she decides to forget him (he is doubtless already married) and look forward to the Ball. As the sisters leave the hotel suite it is of Zdenka and Elemer that the music tells us. Both these are optimistic for their hearts' desire; both will be disappointed — though for Zdenka and for Arabella there is in store a brighter fulfilment than either ever allowed herself to imagine. For Strauss, one may feel, there was an indefinable optimism in the flat keys; some of us may share with him the feeling that, while they adorn the stave, comfort is in store for the soul. The second act opens in such rosy hopes, in B♭ with the first enunciation of the Staircase music, the symbol of a happy end [24].

We are in the anteroom of the main hall in the Hotel Sperl at Leopoldstadt,

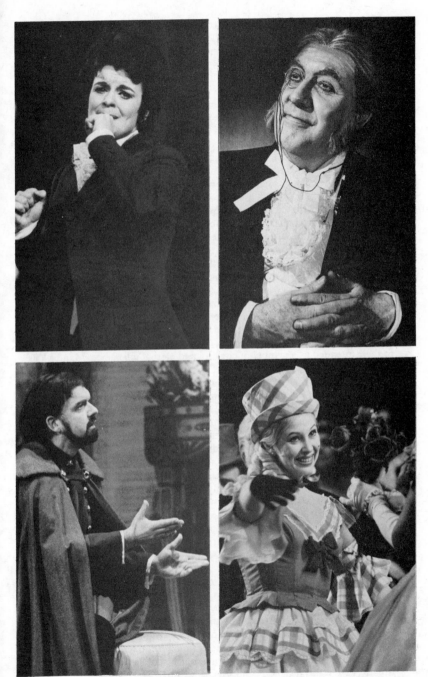

'Arabella' at Covent Garden: Elisabeth Robson as Zdenka, 1967; Michael Langdon as Waldner, 1965; Robert Tear as Matteo, 1977; Elizabeth Harwood as Fiakermilli, 1967 (photos: Royal Opera House Archives, Clive Barda, Reg Wilson)

a district of Vienna, during the Coachmen's Ball on the same evening. Waldner and Mandryka are waiting [23] as Arabella and her mother descend the stairs from the ballroom, surrounded by admirers and themes of gaiety [14] and loveliness [5]. Mandryka presses Waldner's hand with such excitement that the prospective father-in-law fears for his card-playing arm [1 and 2]. Arabella is so awed by the sight of her Right Man that she has to wait alone for a moment before coming down to be presented to Mandryka. The parents tactfully disappear — the admirers have already gone to find new partners. The suitor and his intended are left alone. Both are shy, both know their own minds but seem fearful lest their desires are not the same. They stammer formalities and invitations and confidences while the three 'noble nonentities' in turn come forward to beg the next dance, only to be invited to apply later. Meanwhile Mandryka reveals himself a widower ('Ich habe eine Frau gehabt'), and with a painful deliberation unlocks his feelings for Arabella. For an anxious moment the Wrong Man theme floats by — it is Mandryka's not Arabella's anxiety. He gathers courage so much that Arabella is almost afraid of his ardour. But she regains her composure (helped by the respite of an invitation to dance with the third of her gay cavaliers) and helps Mandryka by revealing her knowledge that he wishes to marry her. He declares it himself, and she reverts to the *Aber der Richtige* music, admitting that her love at first sight was not mistaken. Love flows like a river through her words. Mandryka takes up the image, and recalls a custom of betrothed girls in his village — the idea of bride-winning brings out another theme, for oboes, horns and lower strings, the Slavonic folk-tune of [26]. These girls go down to the river Danube at bedtime, draw a cup of clear water and present it to their intended as a symbol of chastity and eternal allegiance. Mandryka's account, punctuated by horn calls of [7], turns to a theme distinct from [25].

Arabella takes up this melody to express the love that she reciprocates herself. The inner joy which her avowal provokes in Mandryka is outwardly expressed in the wide vocal leaps of [21]. Arabella and Mandryka pledge their troth in a solemn duet [26], whose words 'Und du wirst mein Gebieter sein' look back to the Book of Ruth and her vow to Naomi: 'Whither thou goest, I will go . . . where thou diest, will I die, and there will I be buried.'

There is a quality of naturalness and humanity about this scene that is deeply moving on paper, overwhelmingly so in the theatre. Strauss's orchestral commentary flows as easily and grandly as the Danube through Vienna, and his vocal lines ride it with the expert abandon of well-tried swimmers — though here the metaphor breaks down, since Strauss, who loved dearly the duetting of lyric soprano and high baritone, designed the setting for these voices and made sure that the current would never be too strong for the swimmer's technique. Chiefly, though, the scene derives its special quality from Hofmannsthal, who here struck a vein of poetic dialogue more happily judged, because more realistic, than anywhere in his operas with Strauss. In the most successful passages of the earlier Strauss-Hofmannsthal operas one senses by comparison the weakness of other dialogues where the librettist was aiming too consciously at art; and in this Mandryka-Arabella scene the acute nervous sensibility is the more sharply felt by us at the receiving end because Hofmannsthal has so skilfully judged the dialogue in terms of two fundamentally simple people. Simplicity is Mandryka's natural voice; and Arabella, after cultivating the mask of sophistication as a defence against the outside world, suddenly falls in with her suitor's vocabulary. She expresses herself in the plain language of a girl

Mandryka (John Bröcheler) overhears Zdenka (Gianni Rolandi) giving the key of Arabella's room to Matteo (Keith Lewis); Glyndebourne, 1984: designed by Julia Trevelyan Oman (photo: Guy Gravett)

who knows that sophisticated conceits will simply frighten away the suitor on whom she has set her heart — and who, in finding the direct language of plain words, discovers that she can best express what is in her heart. This quality of highly poetic simplicity is to be felt at the topmost level in her reprise of *Aber der Richtige*, and in the biblical reminiscence of *Und du wirst mein Gebieter sein*. Something of the same direct eloquence pierces through the period language of *Der Rosenkavalier* in the Octavian-Marschallin scenes, especially that with Sophie preceding the final trio. We miss the quality, where we might expect it, in the Barak scenes of *Die Frau ohne Schatten* because Hofmannsthal's sights seem fixed on lofty sentiments which he fears to cheapen by directness. Helen and Menelaus are much more interesting characters than Arabella and Mandryka, but they are infinitely less real and compelling.

When the orchestra has played lovingly with the Betrothal music, Arabella suggests that her intended should return to the hotel while she dances farewell to her girlhood. After a moment's disppointment, expressed only through [13], he gladly grants her freedom for the evening, but insists on remaining

25

where she is. And now the whole party streams into the anteroom, led by Dominik who introduces their spokeswoman, Fiakermilli the coachmen's mascot. She claims Arabella as Queen of the Ball, the brightest star in Vienna, a town with a flair for star-spotting; her solo *Die Wiener Herrn* is a lively florid number, tearing up to top Ds at the drop of a coachman's *Zylinder*, and making appropriate references to Arabella's [5]. Strauss seems to have seized gladly on such a helpful compendium of Zerbinetta and the Adèle of *Die Fledermaus*, at a moment of brilliance and gaiety, and to have given no forethought to the drab vulgarity which the song suggests unless the singer has a trim, jewelled vocal technique and the artistry to convey plebeian fun without musical tastelessness. (This must have been why Clemens Krauss begged the composer to omit the character for the 1942 Salzburg production.) Milli's solo melts into a waltz for dancing. Mandryka and Adelaide exchange a few blissful civilities, simultaneously Zdenka comforts the wretched Matteo as best she can. Adelaide fetches her husband who embraces the saviour of the family fortunes, and they prepare to celebrate.

Here comes Arabella on the arm of Dominik, bidding farewell to the first man who courted her. Elemer succeeds him, full of impetuous optimism; but he too is thanked and sent away, not without protest. Thirdly Lamoral to whom Arabella grants the warmest of the dialogues, musically considered, and crowns it with a loving kiss ([7] in augmentation on the horns almost makes him think he has been chosen) before taking him off for a last waltz. It is the tenderness with which Arabella carries off this process of mass leave-taking that endears to her audience a character not basically as lovable by half as Zdenka. Arabella's personality retains little of the hardness associated with her in *Lucidor*; in the opera libretto she has acquired reserves of affection and gentleness the extent of which it is the story's business to draw out. The two dance away and the orchestra follows them in glamorous waltz tempo with [5] and [14] as suitable counterpoints to elegant waltz tunes. Matteo lurks in the anteroom, and now what seemed a very subsidiary, rather quaint, sub-plot casts shadows over the main action. Mandryka overhears Zdenka giving Matteo a letter purporting to come from Arabella. Matteo (for reasons explained in Hofmannsthal's original libretto to Act One) fears the worst of this. Zdenka persuades him to feel it, and what he feels is the key to Arabella's bedroom — an onomatopoeic theme [27]. Stupid Matteo comments aloud on it, and leaves only just before Mandryka decides to take action, calling his bodyguard Welko to stop Matteo — without success. But Zdenka's deception (it is the key to her own room) is made plain in a strong unison theme for strings [28].

The supper party has begun to assemble; Arabella's hour of leave-taking is not over yet, so that Mandryka is tempted to feel ridiculous in his suspicions, although nagging fears, chiefly concerned with [27], interrupt his attempts at consolation through alcohol (sociable [23]). He sends his servants to search for Arabella throughout the ballroom. One of them returns with a letter from Arabella excusing herself for the rest of the evening. Further inflamed (he asks if the envelope contains a key), Mandryka flings himself into an attempt to get everyone, chiefly himself, thoroughly drunk; and he begins to flirt with Fiakermilli, singing her a savage song, full of sarcastic musical references to [26] and [27], about an incautious lover who loses his girl. Fiakermilli echoes his phrases with nice irony. But Adelaide begins at last to feel concern for Arabella; she is answered roughly by Mandryka, as is her husband, though he puts a practical face on what seems an awkward turn of events and suggests

26

Joan Carlyle as Arabella at Covent Garden, 1970 (photo: Donald Southern)

that they and Mandryka and Waldner's own card-party should return to the hotel to look for Arabella. Mandryka adds [23] that meanwhile those in the ballroom may consider themselves to be his guests. 'Hurrah!' they shout in a coda that is sarcastically jubilant, but customarily omitted, since the Munich version (for a production in 1939 which, by means of a revolving stage, could do a quick stage transformation) plunges into the Prelude to the third act.

The third act opens with an extended Prelude depicting the appointed rendezvous and passage of love between Matteo and Zdenka-would-be-Arabella (what hidden motives here!) with an ardour and realism that yield nothing to the *Rosenkavalier* overture dealing with the same subject. The persistence of Arabella's [5] is obviously in Matteo's mind, but the Prelude is mainly concerned with the six themes of the two parties physically involved.

We see the main hall of the Waldners' hotel, with two flights of stairs ascending to the floor above. Up there Matteo is seen closing the door of what he still believes to be Arabella's room; and when the house bell rings he vanishes.

Arabella enters the hall, themes of Carnival and her Right Man ringing in her head. She sits for a moment in a rocking chair, singing a simple, folk-like ditty (*Über seine Felder*) before preparing to go upstairs to bed. This delectable moment of calm between the storms makes happy references to [22, 26, 18, 4] and two Arabella themes [5, 15], all without a trace of effort. Matteo peeps over the banisters, and is astonished to see Arabella; he can hardly believe (with reason) that she has so quickly and unobservedly come downstairs again; she, on the other hand, is displeased to see him at all. They converse at cross purposes (a good deal of the deceptive [28]) about each other's present and immediately past whereabouts, Matteo proving quite exceptionally inane, even by his own standards. He tries to thank her for what she has granted him; she, of course, is at a loss to explain his gratitude and when pressed with times and places denies that she was upstairs a quarter of an hour previously. Matteo is almost more beside himself than usual when the hotel bell rings and the deputation of family and others enters at rapid tempo. Adelaide complains of the noise in the foyer; Mandryka sees Arabella with that cursed key-man Matteo and orders his servants to pack for the homeward journey. Arabella alone remains calm and firm, upheld by the certainty of [24]. The parents try to dispel the unrest and discontent; Mandryka asks to beg his excuses of Arabella, with financial recompense [23] if necessary. He has lost interest in the marriage since finding her with the object of his firmest suspicions. Arabella pierces through the heavily ambivalent innuendo and asks if Matteo has had any claim on her as strong as that of her fiancé Mandryka. Matteo hesitates and Mandryka's suspicions seem tragically confirmed. His politeness to all and sundry could be cut with a knife. Waldner proposes a duel between himself and Mandryka, but realizes just in time that his pistols are pawned. A crowd of hotel residents collects and a little hushed ensemble ensues. Arabella, urged by Mandryka to admit her complicity, denies with all her strength that Matteo is her lover, and swears that she is telling the truth. Mandryka confronts her with the rendezvous made by her brother on her behalf — she almost divines the explanation, but not quite. The music stops. She refuses to speak further with Mandryka. He is now prepared for a duel with Matteo, and lights a cigarette.

At this moment a voice from the first landing cries for Papa and Mama. Down the stairs comes Zdenka, in a nightdress, her boy's hair suddenly revealed at girl's length (we are never told how this was able to happen, but

Kiri te Kanawa in the title role at Covent Garden in 1977 (photo: Clive Barda)

Mandryka (John Bröcheler) demonstrates to Count Waldner (Artur Korn) how he was attacked by a she-bear; Glyndebourne, 1984 (photo: Guy Gravett)

Waldner (Harold Blackburn) refuses Mandryka's offer of money (Peter Glossop), ENO, 1980 (photo: Clive Barda)

perhaps we had better not ask). Zdenka intends to say farewell to one and all before jumping into the Danube, there to drown her shame. Adelaide, suddenly recognizing the scandal of transvestism, orders her to hold her tongue till death. Waldner gives his wife similar orders, with the reminder that this repays her for her masquerade-making. Zdenka, *in extremis*, tells Arabella what has happened, and reveals her sex to Matteo who has not, even now, guessed the truth; he was destined for a glorious career in the army. Mandryka, on the other hand, could sink through the floor for shame. Arabella calms her sister's fears and, by her personal radiance, has Mandryka almost prostrate before her. He rises and asks Waldner to accept Matteo as a son-in-law (*Brautwerbung kommt*). All is well, as the Staircase theme confirms. Waldner can go back to his cards. Adelaide can lead Zdenka back to bed. Matteo can disappear, as befits his behaviour. The crowd can return to bed or whatever.

Arabella is left with Mandryka; she asks for no more discussion until next morning, but requests that his servant bring her a glass of water to her room, to cool her mind and thirst. The lamps are lowered. Mandryka stands wretched and solitary with his remorse in the hall, a million reproaches and at least half a dozen themes chasing one another round his head.

But the light on the landing suddenly falls on Arabella. The Staircase music begins for the last time, at full stretch, including [7] and other allusions, as she descends holding the glass of water, grace and dedication in her features, Welko quietly following her. It is one of the great moments in all opera, Hofmannsthal's last and perhaps most moving *coup-de-théâtre*, not to be remembered or witnessed without a transport of emotion. Mandryka perceives the exquisite appropriateness and significance of what she is doing (for this is the bridal custom that he taught Arabella in Act Two), and he shrinks from her greatness of soul. As she reaches the bottom step of the staircase, during the descent of which her mouthpiece, Richard Strauss, has confided the thoughts that she and her beloved share, she begins the finale of the opera, '*Das war sehr gut, Mandryka*'. She had thought, she says, to drink the water alone, for purely selfish refreshment, until an ocean of love swept over her as she saw him there in the darkness, and she knew she must leave the drink untouched, and bequeath it to her loved one on this evening when her girlhood finds its end. Mandryka drinks with deep reverence, then smashes the glass on the stone of the staircase. Their betrothal is complete. 'Will you stay as you are?' he begs her. 'I cannot be otherwise,' she answers. 'Take me as I am!' She falls into his loving arms, kisses him goodnight and for the last time runs up the stairs to her solitary room.

When one first gets to know the opera, one wonders if such a flower of the social world could ever live happily ever after on a farming estate. But a careful study of Arabella's character and of the way she expresses herself in her two duet scenes with Mandryka leaves no real doubt that here she has found her ideal level. She knew that flirtation and adulation and rides in the Prater must end as soon as she grew up, and she had decided with a firmness that some girls, and particularly eldest daughters, take upon themselves as their badge of independence that growing-up and taking her own responsibility was her next step in life. Arabella is really quite a simple girl and her pride comes from simple integrity, not from self-preservation (like Christine Storch) nor sophisticated ambition (like the Dyer's wife). She will make Mandryka a perfect gentleman farmer's wife, an ornament to any society, and she will live a life of pure happiness in doing so.

31

Edita Gruberova as Fiakermilli at the Vienna State Opera

A Profound Simplicity

Patrick J. Smith

When Hugo von Hofmannsthal began serious work on his last libretto, *Arabella*, the idea had been in his mind for almost twenty years. He liked to think about ideas a long while before committing them to paper, and even then revised them thoroughly before he was satisfied. Hofmannsthal admitted to being hyper-critical about his plots, and *Arabella* itself underwent over twenty revisions before Hofmannsthal sent even the first draft to Richard Strauss. The difficulty he experienced in the handling of dramatic stagecraft is evidenced by the inadequacy, as viable operatic material, of this much-over-worked draft.

The original idea for *Arabella* was embodied in a short sketch that Hofmannsthal wrote in 1910 entitled *Lucidor, Characters for an Unwritten Comedy*. In this fragment, the focus is not on Arabella but on her sister Lucile, who is portrayed as a tomboy. The father is dead; the mother, Frau von Murska, has arrived from Poland, impoverished, in order to be closer to a rich uncle, who is an eccentric misogynist. Since the very feminine Arabella would be of no interest to him, Frau von Murska dresses the younger girl as a boy, Lucidor.

One of Arabella's admirers is a certain Vladimir, who happens also to be a friend of the uncle's. Arabella ignores him, which arouses Lucile's pity; because of this Lucile writes Vladimir a love letter, forging the hand of her sister. Vladimir, who up to now has only had a passing interest in Arabella, becomes infatuated as the letters continue, while Arabella in public ignores him in preference to the socially inferior Herr von Imfanger. Lucile finally gives herself to Vladimir in a darkened room — not once but several times — and the sketch ends when Lucile reveals her deception to Vladimir and Arabella.

The irony is that what is most believable in *Lucidor* becomes, because of a shift not only of focus but of medium, least believable in *Arabella*. Lucile in boy's clothes is shown as the all-feminine in opposition to her beautiful sister, who wears her femininity as a cloak to hide her pettiness. But in the opera Arabella has become the focal character and far more a complete woman than a coquette. She has therefore pre-empted Lucile's position. In the opera, Zdenka (the Lucile figure) is no longer of central importance, and we are shown her character *in medias res*, with no chance to witness the growing of her love. Similarly, Matteo (the Vladimir figure) is also seen *in medias res*, for in *Lucidor* he grew to love Arabella precisely because of 'her' letters to him — before that he had only been mildly interested in her. In *Arabella*, however, Matteo is in love with the person Arabella, and the letters have served merely to inflame him further. In the sketch, Hofmannsthal was developing a triangle situation with easily comprehended affinities, whereas in the opera he had the more difficult task of defining and differentiating two sympathetic couples. Finally, Hofmannsthal through the means of the misogynic uncle — who is not in the opera — was able to give a far more plausible reason for having a girl in boy's clothes, as well as being able to portray her disguise more believably than under the glare of the stage lights. It is not surprising, therefore, that the final libretto of *Arabella* is flawed insofar as it depends on aspects of *Lucidor*, and is superior when it has been superseded by his later development of the story.

I have begun with a discussion of *Lucidor* because it well reflects the problems that Hofmannsthal had with the story; problems that continued as he developed it for Strauss. The draft first act he sent Strauss highlights the extent of his difficulties, for it is a confused and over-busy work, which merited Strauss's strictures. 'Over this comic opera we have got ourselves into an awkward spot for the first time in our lives,' Hofmannsthal wrote, and it was the revision of that first act that he sent to Strauss just before he died.

The strength of *Arabella* as an opera lies not in its stagecraft, which is imperfect. From a visual point of view, the girl in boy's clothes will always pose a problem in a genre work of this sort. From a plotting point of view, the scene in which Mandryka overhears Zdenka giving Matteo the key to Arabella's room is both weak and unbelievable, as is, from a characterizational viewpoint, Mandryka's insensate response (however well Hofmannsthal tries to justify it in terms of Mandryka's memory of a perfect first wife and his suspicion of the mores of the Viennese). Lastly, the notion that Matteo can have sexual relations with a woman — even in a pitch-black room — he thinks he deeply loves and not realize the deception is best passed over in silence. These are usually the specifics mentioned by those who ridicule the opera, just as those who dislike the music compare it unfavourably to *Rosenkavalier*.

The truth is that *Arabella* has a stature well beyond the inadequacies of its specifics, simply because it is one of the very few mature comedies of manners in operatic history. Hofmannsthal, that master of characterizational subtlety, operated here on his finest level of achievement, and Strauss's music, though never equalling the subtlety of Hofmannsthal's liquid and evocative poetry, provided a rich and lyric frame within which the comedy could be realized. It is, of course, a pity that Hofmannsthal did not live to collaborate on the opera as Strauss set it to music (Strauss himself refused to change Hofmannsthal's text out of respect), but what we are given nonetheless is a work whose humanity grants it a special place in the affections of many operagoers.

Arabella is the story of growing up: of the growing into womanhood of two sisters, of the growing into understanding first of Arabella and Mandryka and second — and to a lesser extent — of all the major characters. It is the story of the moment when the impetuosity and exuberance of youth becomes the forgiving wisdom of maturity; of the moment of true love and of that moment made permanent. It is a story where heart and head become one in wisdom and emotion: a story in whose ending there is but a beginning — the future. In that sense *Arabella* is a fairy tale.

Hofmannsthal had little patience for the kind of unbridled passion represented by *Tristan and Isolde*, feeling that passion has to be combined with an awareness of others and a *caritas* of friendship as well as sexual love to become in any sense permanent. His other librettos — *Die Frau ohne Schatten* in particular, but even *Die Aegyptische Helena*, with its concept of a couple 'vollvermählt' (fully married) — are inextricably involved with this concept of a human progress — a progress which refers, in operatic history, back to that of Tamino and Pamina in *The Magic Flute*. The fire and water here are Arabella and Mandryka's realisations, in the third act, that their dreams of the perfect spouse are chimeric, and that human life must include not only the dream but the reality, which necessarily involves understanding and forgiveness. The famous glass of pure spring water which is the central symbol of *Arabella*, and which is the excuse for one of Strauss's greatest final scenes, is thus neither a simplistic one-for-one symbol nor a cheap stage trick. As Hofmannsthal wrote to Strauss: 'Instead of any ceremony at this point,

Gianni Rolandi as Zdenka and Ashley Putnam as Arabella at Glyndebourne in 1984. Producer John Cox, designer Julia Trevelyan Oman (photo: Guy Gravett)

one could of course have the still outstanding engagement kiss. Yet this simple ceremony of carrying the filled glass down the stairs has immense mimic advantages. A kiss she cannot carry *towards* him, she would simply have to walk up to him and give him the kiss; the other implies the most bridal gesture in its chastest form . . .' Thus the glass of water contains within its symbolism the freight of the three acts of the opera, and it represents acceptance and forgiveness at once. It is significant, moreover, that in her speech to Mandryka Arabella says: 'And thus this drink that none has touched I offer to my friend this evening when I'm parting from the girl that I have been' — using the word 'friend' and not 'beloved'. Passion and liking have become fused, and thus a lasting relationship can be founded.

It is no accident that *Arabella* takes place on the final day of festival before Lent: the Cabmen's Ball of which Arabella is queen represents the final moment of her irresponsible youth. Arabella realises what it signifies, and she knows she must sacrifice herself to her family, if necessary, and decide on one of her suitors. It is this sense of responsibility toward others that Strauss felt was inadequately shown in earlier drafts, and which he and Hofmannsthal felt must be clearly portrayed if Arabella was to emerge as more than a coquette. Mandryka's offstage presence, sensed as soon as Arabella enters, represents her last chance of the kind of fairy-tale romance she has been dreaming of, and which she knows that none of the known suitors will provide. Hofmannsthal's irony is that her wild surmise that this will be an instant love match will be in fact realised, but will, almost as fast, be wrecked, so that Arabella will have to re-create that love on a more lasting basis.

Lucia Popp as Zdenka and Gundula Janowitz as Arabella at the Vienna State Opera

The early part of the first act contrasts the two sisters. This was important for, once Arabella became the focus, it was vital that Zdenka be differentiated from her. Thus the all-giving nature of the younger sister is brought strongly to the fore and is then contrasted with Arabella's more self-possessed femininity.

In their celebrated duet, Arabella dreams selfishly about a 'right man', while Zdenka, 'looking at her lovingly', responds with no thought for herself but only for Arabella's happiness — and it is significant that Strauss, at this point, seized on the moment to interpolate a folk melody. The melody, then, acts as a ground bass unifying the two sisters, while giving the duet a melodic shape, and the contrasting timbres and vocal lines of the two sopranos both complement and enhance this moment, highlighting in music the two-in-one nature of the emotional scene. Strauss would use the same technique for similar results in the love duet of the second act.

Hofmannsthal's strengths as a playwright and as a sensitive psychologist are at their finest in the scene between Mandryka and Count Waldner. This is never given the consideration of the more famous vocal passages in the score. I think that in part this lack of attention, as in several other psychologically subtle scenes, is owing to Strauss's music.

There is no doubt that Strauss had a melodic gift, an ability to write for the female voice and the ability to spin out of a few notes a web of glorious music. But what he lacked was the quickness of psychological response that illuminates a character in music in a few bars. Strauss used the leitmotif technique of Wagner extensively — and it is employed in *Arabella* — but, though the themes give a general shape of the character — its outward form — they never penetrate the skin. A brilliant example of leitmotif as character portrait — that of Gutrune, in *Twilight of the Gods* — was beyond Strauss's abilities. Similarly, in intimate scenes such as the Mandryka/Waldner one, he is unable to highlight in music the many subtle shadings of Hofmannsthal's text, as the two men get to know each other. Strauss blocks in the scene with broad strokes, and he knows exactly what to do with the splendid finale, as

Waldner, now suddenly rich because of Mandryka's largesse with his wallet, repeats the phrase 'Teschek, bedien dich' ('Take some, I mean it') in several ways, dances around the amazed Zdenka and out of the door. The ending, of course, is analogous — visually at least — to that which ends Act Two of *Rosenkavalier*, and almost as stage effective.

Arabella's monologue, which closes the first act, is the place where the shadow of *Rosenkavalier* falls most heavily. The text presents her awareness of her duty, her lack of feeling for Elemer and Matteo and, significantly, her realisation of her sister's personality. Strauss rather dutifully sets it, but there is not that quick of identification that is present at the end of the first act of *Rosenkavalier*. The pith of the act, we feel, has come earlier.

The second act opens with an expectant, swelling chord, and leads to the Arabella/Mandryka scene. Attention has again been confined to the love duet that is its centre, although Hofmannsthal here created a courtship ritual in miniature. Arabella's opening statement is superficially naive, but in fact both coquettish and sophisticated: 'You don't look like someone who would care about all this. I wonder what brought you here?', which flusters Mandryka and throws him off-guard. He responds, eventually, with his true character of gruff and direct honesty, and this in turn startles Arabella. Hofmannsthal has been careful to differentiate Mandryka's passionate certitude from Elemer's impetuous demands, and it is this conviction that wins her over and leads to Mandryka's explanation of the drink of pure water which is a betrothal custom in his village — and which, as Hofmannsthal realizes, will instantly appeal to Arabella's yearning for a fairy-tale romance. Time and again it is Hofmannsthal's acuteness of character portrayal that persuades us to believe in these people, despite the vicissitudes of the plot.

Arabella then asks to stay on at the ball, and Mandryka busies himself with ordering champagne and flowers. What follows is one of the most touching scenes in the opera (and rare in all opera): Arabella's farewell to her suitors. It

Arabella (Josephine Barstow) bids goodbye to Count Lamoral (Roderick Earle), ENO, 1980 (photo: Clive Barda)

37

is the test of a great rather than merely a vocally effective Arabella, for the soprano must differentiate her response to the three Counts: tender to her first suitor, Dominik, with the tenderness of nostalgia, firm to the angry, frustrated and spluttering Elemer, and wistful — and not a little sad — to the gentle Lamoral, whom she kisses on the forehead and grants a final waltz.

It is not surprising that the episode of the key, of Mandryka's eavesdropping and consequent (and entirely characteristic) descent into rage and drunkenness did not summon Strauss's complete musical attention. Strauss, for all his technical abilities as a composer, was straightforward in his approach to music, and if he did not feel the texts he was setting would simply cover them with wellmade music of a perfectly acceptable sort, but which had little inner urgency. Thus in the rest of the act Strauss the composer does not 'rescue' Hofmannsthal the craftsman (as, it can be argued, Weber 'rescued' his librettists for *Euryanthe* and *Oberon*).

The third act is usually thought of in terms of its close, which is its musical highlight and, leaving aside the quite different case of *Salome*, the first of the series of soprano closing scenes that would continue with *Daphne* and *Capriccio*. And yet that moment, inspired musically and verbally as it is, is merely the seal which is set upon the events of self-awareness and reconciliation. What has occurred earlier is the centre of the act, and the true centre of the drama.

It begins, of course, with the cross-purposes encounter between the still-bedazzled and dreamy Arabella, and the equally bedazzled Matteo. When the group from the ball arrives Mandryka is confirmed in his opinion of Arabella's betrayal. As the misunderstanding develops, Hofmannsthal's character studies are at their best. Arabella does not crumble into tears or hysteria but shows her strength in response to Mandryka's barely controlled fury; she stands her ground. On another level, Waldner is desperately trying to patch over the situation, for three reasons: he does not want to see abrogated this heaven-sent marriage, which will end his financial worries; he does not want the quarrel to end, as he sees it might, in a duel with Mandryka that he cannot as a father refuse; and, most immediately, he wants to get back to his card game. Countess Waldner, for her part, is trying to save the situation by accusing Matteo.

It is here that Arabella says something which should not have been lost in the musical fabric. She has retained a dignity in the face of inexplicable events. This is the quality that others, including her sister, have found heartless — yet it is the quality that makes her most womanly and most memorable. 'What good is anything in this world if this man is so weak that he hasn't the strength to believe me?'

Hofmannsthal has finished with his portrayal of idyllic love, and he is now moving to something far more important in human terms: understanding through love. Arabella has begun to realise that her dream prince — 'the right man' — is a mortal like everyone else, and must be accepted faults and all. Although Hofmannsthal considered this scene the focus of the evening, Strauss directed his musical attention to the culmination — the final scene — and more or less slid over this part of the act. It is all the more a pity that Hofmannsthal died when he did, for had he lived he might have been able to get Strauss to highlight the changes taking place, first in Arabella and then in Mandryka.

Zdenka's appearance in a negligée means the deceptions are over. Arabella senses the truth and immediately acts: she chooses to stand by Zdenka in her

Adelaide (Shelagh Squires) chivvies Zdenka (Norma Burrows) up the stairs in the last act of the 1980 ENO production (photo: Clive Barda)

Kiri te Kanawa in the title role, Covent Garden, 1981 (photo: Clive Barda)

disgrace. Mandryka now realises what he has done, and goes up to Arabella to apologise. The dream prince has become human, and is learning humility. What is taking place in Mandryka is what has been taking place in Arabella during the past quarter hour: the realisation that one lives in this world not only for oneself and for one's own pleasures and desires, and that in any mutual relationship there must be mutual compromise.

Not looking at Mandryka, Arabella speaks to Zdenka in what for her is the key speech of the whole opera: 'Zdenkerl, you're so much kinder than I am./You have a heart more loving than mine, and nothing counts for you,/nothing in this world but what your heart may bid you do./I thank you, dear, you've given me a golden lesson:/it's not for us to want things, to demand them — / we must not weigh, we must not trade, nor ever stint,/but give and love till the day we die.' The sentiment is romantic, as always with Arabella, but it is the romanticism, now, of awareness.

The roles of Arabella and Mandryka have been reversed. It is now Arabella who is the stronger and who must lead her beloved. This moment is Arabella's triumph — the saving of herself and of her impending marriage — and it is the justification of her central position in the opera. And yet the actress must be careful not to dominate Mandryka at this point, for Hofmannsthal realised that true marriage was the combination of the strengths of man and woman.

Yet this passage is quite often cut because Strauss wrote less than memorable music for it. Nowhere is it more evident that Strauss did not understand the shape of the final act than here, and it takes a masterly performance by the Arabella to force recognition of it.

Mandryka instinctively senses that it is up to him to make an act of apology beyond mere words (this is Hofmannsthal the psychological dramatist at his finest), and he asks Waldner to grant Matteo Zdenka's hand. Since poor Matteo has not yet said that he is in love with Zdenka, this act is to say the least precipitous, but it is psychologically correct, for in standing up for Matteo Mandryka is actually asking Arabella's forgiveness.

That forgiveness is withheld until the final scene. We are not given Arabella's state of mind as she went upstairs, received the glass of water and decided to return, although she says that she only intended to drink it and go to bed. This is too easy an explanation, even if she believes it: she knows the implications of the glass of water for Mandryka. Perhaps she willed herself not to think of it; perhaps she intended (as Mandryka said) to drink it as a gesture of revenge for his lack of trust in her and then see what the morrow would bring. What matters is that she received the glass, saw her beloved standing in the darkness below, and realised once more and finally that it was up to her to make the last gesture of forgiveness and love. She has no other course open, and she descends the stairs.

One of Hofmannsthal's aphorisms goes: 'Depth must be hidden. Where? On the surface.' *Arabella* is the exegesis of that aphorism, and Arabella's last sentence is its vindication. The simplicity of 'I can do no other, take me as I am!', which contains within it the whole of the preceding drama, is the simplicity and purity of the last scene, symbolized in the glass of pure water. The lovers (including Zdenka and her Matteo) will spend the rest of their lives in the realisation of its meaning. The moment, the poetry, the music are one, and the one is perfect in its humanity.

Arabella is not faultless but few, if any, operas can be said to express so profound and so beautiful a loving understanding of human nature. The achievement is Hofmannsthal's, and the achievement is Strauss's.

Two scenes from 'Arabella' at ENO: Act Two, with Rosemary Ashe as Fiakermilli, 1984;
Act Three with Harold Blackburn as Waldner and Peter Glossop as Mandryka, 1980
(photos: Clive Barda)

Hofmannsthal's Last Libretto

Karen Forsyth

In 1906 Strauss and Hofmannsthal began work on *Elektra*, their first opera. In 1927 *Arabella*, the sixth and last, was begun. On July 15, 1929 Hofmannsthal died of a stroke at the age of fifty-five at his house in Rodaun outside Vienna, while getting ready to attend the funeral of his son Franz, who had committed suicide two days earlier. The libretto to *Arabella* was complete, though it is clear that Hofmannsthal would still have revised the second and third acts. Obviously he never heard the finished score, which received its première in Dresden on July 1, 1933.

Hofmannsthal's death was brought on by shock and grief. This sensitive, highly-strung, introspective man was less well-equipped than most to withstand such a blow. Son of a Viennese bank director, of mixed Bavarian, Austrian, Italian and Jewish stock, he was brought up a Roman Catholic and kept that faith until his death. (He was buried in the habit of a Franciscan monk.) Hofmannsthal was a true son of the Austro-Hungarian Empire; its cosmopolitanism, its exoticism, its dreamlike glamour and decadence drew him and held him fast. As his friend Rudolf Borchardt said of him, 'In his spiritual realm the sun never sets.' Phenomenally gifted as a boy, reputed to be master of seven languages, he soon moved with precocious assurance in this intoxicating atmosphere, while in adulthood it was with a consciously thought-out set of ethical beliefs that he tried to contain the vast amoral flux within him. When the crash came and the Empire began to collapse, eventually to leave Austria an insignificant country one-eighth its former size, Hofmannsthal was young and resilient enough to counter the event with this same sense of duty. In 1915 he worked in counter-intelligence as a sort of cultural-political attaché delivering addresses throughout Europe. In his role as 'Kulturpolitiker' he set up a series of studies on Austrian history and literature called *Österreichische Bibliothek* (*Austrian Library*), published six essays on related topics and, after the war, with Max Reinhardt and Richard Strauss, founded the Salzburg Festival to help preserve Austria's cultural influence in a newly-created Europe. But in the long term, and as he grew older, the shock of Austria's loss of power was more profound than Hofmannsthal at first realized. He felt himself increasingly displaced and was increasingly prone to depressive illness. Three years before his death he wrote to Carl J. Burckhardt: 'For me Vienna is a place I find very difficult to bear . . . the current situation is something only a stranger can take, for me it is *petrifying* . . . For you the whole thing is a theatrical decoration and speaks to you of things that are dead but for you that is one charm the more. For me almost everything is *terrifying*.' (*Hugo von Hofmannsthal-Carl J. Burckhardt: Correspondence*, October 25, 1926.) His son's death was thus a personal tragedy which concentrated beyond endurance his larger sense of loss.

Strauss, it is true, was equally rooted in the past, equally conservative; but his situation was different. In the first place he was favoured with a more robust and serene temperament; and in the second, for him the past meant essentially the German musical past, dominated by Mozart and Wagner. His only duty was to continue to work within this tradition. This is not the place to argue about Strauss's apolitical view of art (or indeed, the apolitical nature of music), beyond remarking, without irony, that it was inseparable from his serenity as an artist.

So it is hardly surprising, given Hofmannsthal's concern for post-war Austria, that *Arabella* began life as a 'second *Rosenkavlier*'. On September 8, 1923 Strauss wrote: 'You'll just *have to write that for me some day* [his italics]: I haven't spoken my last word yet in that genre. Something delicate, amusing and warm-hearted!' This evidently prompted Hofmannsthal to take out his old short story *Lucidor* (1910). (Typical of Hofmannsthal is that he had in the intervening years tried to rework the material in different genres; in this case, comedy, vaudeville and film.) The plot of the earlier story, which had some origins in Molière, now provided him almost exactly with the Arabella – Zdenka (= Lucidor) – Matteo configuration, with the notable difference that the earlier Arabella is a cold-hearted creature without a love of her own. When it came to writing the libretto Hofmannsthal largely used notes to an unwritten *Lucidor* comedy, in which the character of Arabella is cast in yet another light. But the fifth opera, *Die Aegyptische Helena* (*The Egyptian Helen*), intervened, and *Lucidor* was laid by.

Scarcely was the ink of *Die Aegyptische Helena* dry than in mid-1927 Strauss called urgently for the next libretto, making in passing some suggestions including an unfortunate one for a kind of autobiographical *Meistersinger*. Hofmannsthal greeted this with derision. After a period of tension, the customary prelude to a new opera, Hofmannsthal took out notes to a fragmentary 'conversation piece' *Der Fiaker als Graf (The Cabby as Count)*, begun in 1927. The notes are extremely thin, almost elliptical, but in a letter to Strauss of October 1, 1927 Hofmannsthal describes it as a light-hearted romance focussing on that old Viennese tradition, the cabbies' ball:

> Two years ago I occupied myself with a comedy, made notes and drafted a scenario, and then I put this work aside again. It was called *The Cabby as Count* . . . It was quite attractive as a subject, but in the end I found there was not enough to it if it was to be done in contemporary dress. The situation of the whole piece was still entirely true in my youth (so long as the court and the aristrocracy meant everything in Vienna); today it would have to be switched back in point of time: I did think of the eighteen-eighties, or even of the eighteen-sixties . . . Last night it occurred to me that this comedy might perhaps be done for music, with the text in a light vein, largely in telegram style.

Hofmannsthal goes on to point out the affinity with *Der Rosenkavalier*.

Clearly *Arabella* as we know it was just within his grasp, and on November 13, 1927 he describes how he intends to combine motives from the two earlier sources:

> . . . I have been able to combine several features of this cabbies' world with elements from another projected comedy and hope . . . to have invented the scenario for a three-act comic opera, indeed almost an operetta (I would describe *Rosenkavalier* as an operetta too!) which in gaiety does not fall short of *Fledermaus*, is kindred to *Rosenkavalier*, without any self-repetition, and contains five or six very lively parts.

So *Arabella* is an opera about Vienna and about Viennese life at a particular period (the 1860s) and it was Hofmannsthal's last tribute to that city. In fact *Arabella* is among the few Hofmannsthal works (*Der Schwierige — The Difficult Man —* is another) in which a specific historical period is allowed to

Lillian Watson as Fiakermilli at Covent Garden, 1981 (photo: Clive Barda)

Act Two at (above) Covent Garden, 1965 and (below) ENO, 1980 (photos: Houston Rogers, Theatre Museum and Clive Barda)

stand without serving as a spring-board to a timeless mythical world; this is, of course, the *only* possible treatment of time in the well-made three-act comedy of manners that *Arabella* is. The danger in *Arabella* is not that the period disappears in a vapour of Hofmannsthalian symbols but that period and place may seem no more than a set of quaint customs and colourful costumes, a kind of hollow 'operatic' locale. In trying to bring in *three* distinct worlds in *Arabella* — that is, the ball, the Waldners' *déclassé* hotel, and the whiff of wild Croatia through the character of Mandryka — it is arguable that Hofmannsthal had bitten off more than even the most experienced librettist could chew.

It was clearly with the *Fiaker als Graf*, section that he ran the greatest risk of sinking into the merely picturesque. How did he become interested in such a subject? In the first half of the 1920s, as part of his general cultural campaign, Hofmannsthal tried to revive interest in the old Viennese popular theatre ('Volkstheater'). His *Xenodoxus*, for example, envisages a part for the 'Kasperl', the Viennese clown. In the *Fiaker als Graf*, which he first called the *Fiaker als Marquis* (*Cabby as Marquis*), it seems that he was aiming at a synthesis of the popular play and the life of that very Viennese institution the ball (focal point of numerous operas and operettas, not only *Die Fledermaus*). Hofmannsthal was always thorough in his study of sources and read Alexander von Weilen's *History of the Viennese Theatre from Earliest Times until the Beginning of the Court Theatres*, also a collection of texts from the popular theatre in the first half of the eighteenth century, and an example of a popular play with the title *Der Fiaker als Marquis*, by Adolf Bäuerle, from which he took nothing but his share in the tradition of comedies about Viennese cabbies. Emanuel Schikaneder, librettist of *The Magic Flute* no less, wrote two, entitled respectively *Die Fiaker in Wien* and *Die Fiaker in Baden* (*The Cabbies in Vienna* and *The Cabbies in Baden*).

Hofmannsthal set his *Arabella* at a time when, on the grounds of immorality, public cabbies' balls had been forbidden in Vienna for about thirty years. Instead they flourished as private balls and in the relative economic prosperity of the 1860s attracted a large and loose demi-monde — who would have been all too ready to deceive a naive Croatian magnate such as Mandryka. Hofmannsthal's ball, with its mixture of historical characters (Fiakermilli) with fictional, of respectability with a degree of debauchery, is something of his own devising, though not far from fact. But what one imagines as the strong 'Cockney' flavour of the cabbies' world is sadly diluted in its final form (for example, Milli's wordless yodelling). The whole effect is rather vapid.

On the other hand the milieu of Count Waldner and his family rings true. It supplies a very poignant background to the problems of emerging adolescent sexuality, though in the earlier fragments the underlying criticism of Viennese social oddities and *laissez-aller* eccentricities is sharper. Arabella herself, in *Lucidor*, has a sharper tongue and a sharper sense of injustice; her pre-marital flirtations seem less harmless. What she gains in statuesque purity in the opera she loses in astringency. The rest of the family take on their operatic selves without discomfort, and the *travesti* is ready-made. The fortune-teller is, of course, pure operetta.

The third world in *Arabella* is that of Mandryka and his Croatian retinue. It is not known what precisely, if anything, prompted Hofmannsthal to make his hero a Croat, but it is evident from the correspondence that he set great store by him. On November 20, 1927 he described Mandryka as a figure 'from

47

a half-foreign world (Croatia), half a *buffo* and at the same time a splendid fellow, someone who feels deeply, is volatile, wild and gentle — almost demoniacal'. In his usual fashion he made a thorough study of sources, in particular of *Folksongs of the Slavs: Selected, translated, introduced and annotated by Paul Eisner* (Leipzig, 1926). Eisner was a Slav scholar and musician with whom Hofmannsthal was in touch and with whom he corresponded on the projected use of folksong in *Arabella*. In the event, he took the names of Mandryka's servants from the titles of some songs, a small number of Slav expressions and some minor linguistic details (such as making the gender of the Danube masculine instead of the usual feminine), and some verses from Slav folksongs, principally those for Mandryka's song in Act Two 'Gieng durch einen Wald, weiss nicht durch welchen' ('I went through a wood, I don't know which one').

If it is not known what actually persuaded Hofmannsthal to make Mandryka a Croat it is possible to suggest reasons why he should have done so. He is, on one level, living evidence of the far-flung reaches of the Danube monarchy. At another level Croatia symbolizes all the virtues of wild untrammelled nature as opposed to the corruption of the city: Mandryka, the naive and virtuous countryman, is its representative.

But there is a third reason why Hofmannsthal made him, so to speak, an 'exotic': his exoticism masks a deficiency in the dramatic construction of the main plot. As Strauss noticed very early on, Arabella herself experiences virtually no conflict at all. He did not care for her and wrote (albeit of the first draft of Act One, later quite extensively revised):

> And then Arabella: does she really do anything particularly exciting? She doesn't love Matteo from the start; as for her flirtation with the three Counts, who display no particular personality in any way, I think you probably overrate its poetical effect... That she still wants to dance a little on her last evening, with [Mandryka's] permission — why, that happens in the best families. (July 23, 1928)

It is true that Arabella's only trial is to endure for a brief hour her lover's unfounded jealousy. The plot is made marginally more interesting if stated from her father's point of view, namely as the rough passage of his scheme to pay off some gambling debts! But the *Arabella* libretto is not as insipid as an outline of the main plot would lead one to believe. Once again it was Strauss who was quick to point out that 'A real conflict exists only in the subsidiary plot between Matteo and Zdenka' (July 23, 1928). In the psychology and the sexual ambiguity of the character Zdenka there is indeed strong and unusual conflict; the sub-plot is far more powerful than the main plot and the link between them is not a necessary one. All that is needed is a peg to hang Mandryka's jealous suspicions on. The sub-plot has the further merit of being as naturally a product of its time and place as was the *Rosenkavalier* plot of an earlier age.

It seems fairly certain that Hofmannsthal, without perhaps admitting it openly, was aware of this. His solution was not, as Strauss suggested (July 23, 1928), to spice things up by letting Arabella's mother flirt with one of the Counts, but was an altogether more static, one might even say Hofmannsthalian, one: that of letting Arabella's and Mandryka's love itself do duty as a plot. We, the audience, are supposed to be so spell-bound by their virtuous affection and its inevitable 'rightness' that we close an eye to its improbable beginnings and the — relative — smoothness of its course

Dietrich Fischer-Dieskau as Mandryka at Covent Garden, 1965 (photo: Houston Rogers, Theatre Museum)

towards a happy ending. Up to a point all this can be excused as falling within the conventions of fairy-tale romance but, however judged, it is clearly all much easier if Mandryka is strongly exotic because he is then less individual, more magically irresistible as a suitor — and more of a symbolic counter-weight to 'Vienna'. Yet all the same, though endowed by the author with some lovable, human attributes, the unavoidable consequence is that Mandryka is little more than an assemblage of arbitrarily selected characteristics. While the text is arguably the best constructed of all Hofmannsthal's librettos, by putting the emphasis on the falling in love — without much falling — Hofmannsthal deprived some of his characters of a full measure of life and drama. Because of this, perhaps, he failed to call forth consistently great music from his composer.

His motives in writing *Arabella* were mixed; he wanted to conserve, celebrate, recreate and even criticize a piece of the Viennese past. There was nothing wrong in this — one might even say that there is a very good libretto, '*Zdenka*', inside *Arabella*, waiting to get out and do just that. If *Arabella* is less biting, less frivolous, larger, blander, and treads on less delicate ground, this may well be because Hofmannsthal's sense of patriotic loyalty would not let him treat certain subjects on such a public platform as opera, nor indeed may he have wished to share them, even with Strauss, with whom, contrary to gossip then and since, he was very close. He opted instead, perhaps with a shade of Viennese nostalgic resignation, for the warm glow of romance, naturally with an ethical Hofmannsthalian core, and in this he could hope with some confidence to speak to the heart of a composer such as Strauss.

Thematic Guide

Many of the themes have been identified by William Mann in his article by numbers in square brackets, which refer to the themes set out on these pages. The themes are also identified by the numbers in square brackets at the corresponding points in the libretto, so that the words can be related to the musical themes.

[10c]

[11]

[12]

f *espr.*

[13]

[14]

[15]

[16]

etc.

p

pp

[17]

p

[18]

[19]

tr

51

[20]

espr.

[21]

pp espr.

[22]

[23]

Take some, I mean it!
Tes-chek, be dien dich!

[24]

p

[25]

pp

[26]

pp

[27]

sf   sf   etc.

[28]

f

Arabella

A Lyrical Comedy in Three Acts
by Richard Strauss

Libretto by Hugo von Hofmannsthal
English translation by John Gutman

Arabella was first performed at the Opernhaus, Dresden, on July 1, 1933. The first performance in England was at Covent Garden on May 17, 1934. The first performance in the United States was at the Metropolitan Opera House, New York, in 1955.

Alexander Young as Matteo and Lisa della Casa as Arabella at Covent Garden, 1965 (photo: Anthony Crickmay)

CHARACTERS

Count Waldner *a Captain in the cavalry, now retired*	bass
Adelaide *his wife*	mezzo-soprano
Arabella ⎫ *their daughters*	soprano
Zdenka ⎭	soprano
Mandryka	baritone
Matteo *an officer*	tenor
Count Elemer ⎫	tenor
Count Dominik ⎬ *admirers of Arabella*	baritone
Count Lamoral ⎭	bass
Fiakermilli	coloratura soprano
A Fortune-teller	soprano
Welko *a hussar, Mandryka's batman*	
Djura ⎫ *Mandryka's servants*	
Jankel ⎭	
A Waiter	
Arabella's Companion	
Three Gamblers	
A Physician	
A Groom	
Coachmen, Guests at the Ball, Hotel Residents, Waiters	

Place: Vienna — Time: 1860

Act One

A drawing-room in a Vienna hotel, richly appointed and newly furnished in the style of the 1860s. Adelaide is seated at a table, opposite the fortune-teller. Zdenka, in boy's clothes, is seated at another table, busy with all kinds of papers.

FORTUNE-TELLER
[1, 2]

The cards are more auspicious than they were last week.

Die Karten fallen besser als das letzte Mal.

ADELAIDE

I hope they are.

Das gebe Gott!

There is a knock at the door.

We cannot be disturbed.

Nur keine Störung jetzt!

ZDENKA
(answers the knock; somebody hands her a letter at the door)

My father is not here, my mother has a headache.
Come again later! One more bill we haven't paid yet.

Mein Vater ist nicht hier, die Mutter hat Migräne.
Kommen Sie später. — Es ist wieder eine Rechnung!

ADELAIDE
(shaking her head)

Not now! Put it down there.

[3] Jetzt nicht! Leg' sie dorthin!

ZDENKA

At least it will have company!

Es liegen schon so viele da!

ADELAIDE

Still, child. What do the cards say? Tell me!
I'm so upset and worried I can't sleep at night.

Still, still! — Wie liegen unsere Karten?
Die Sorge und die Ungeduld verzehren mich!

FORTUNE-TELLER
(pondering over her cards)

No need to worry now . . . inheritance approaching . . . but slowly.

Beruhigen Sie sich. Die Erbschaft rückt schon näher — nur langsam!

ADELAIDE
(in despair)

No! We cannot wait much longer.
The only hope that's left us —
immediate marriage for our Arabella.

Nein, wir können nicht mehr warten!
Es gibt nur eine Hoffnung:
[4] die baldige Vermählung unserer Arabella!

FORTUNE-TELLER

I see her father — it's your husband whom I see.
Bad luck is at his side . . . around him it is dark.
He fights . . . with cards — dear me!

And once again he's losing a lot of money.

Den Vater seh ich, Ihren Herrn Gemahl —
o weh, die Sorge steht ihm nah — ganz
[1] finster ist's um ihn.
[2] Er kämpft, er spielt — o weh, und er verspielt schon wieder
die grosse Summe.

ADELAIDE

Mighty Lord in Heaven [3, 4]
come to my rescue through my lovely child!

Heil'ge Mutter Gottes!
Komm mir zu Hilfe durch mein schönes Kind!

55

Go on, and tell me; this engagement — is it [5, 9] Um Gottes willen, die Verlobung — ist sie
near? nah?
Even our credit isn't what it used to be. Unser Kredit ist sehr im Wanken, liebste
Frau!

FORTUNE-TELLER
(after another long look at her cards)

An officer I see ... Da steht der Offizier.

ADELAIDE

That's not so good, I fear. [6] Ein Offizier? o weh!

ZDENKA
(aside)

Matteo! Matteo!

FORTUNE-TELLER

But ... I do not think he is the one. [7, 8, 4] Nein! der ist der Eigentliche nicht!

ADELAIDE

I should not hope so! Das will ich hoffen!

FORTUNE-TELLER

It seems a stranger comes from over Von dort herüber kommt der fremde Herr,
there ... the fiancé. der Bräutigam.

ADELAIDE

My brooch with pearls and rubies shall be Die Brosche mit Smaragden ist Ihr
your reward Eigentum, wenn
if what you have predicted should come Ihre Prophezeiung Wahrheit wird in dieser
true before next Sunday. Woche!

FORTUNE-TELLER
(slowly, as though deciphering the book of fate)

He comes from very far ... Er kommt von weiter her.

ADELAIDE

From very far? Von weiter her?

FORTUNE-TELLER

He's summoned by a letter. Ein Brief hat ihn gerufen.

ADELAIDE

It is Count Elemer — that's obvious! Es ist Graf Elemer, kein Zweifel!

FORTUNE-TELLER

I see a forest with its trees — that's where Ich sehe einen grossen Wald: dort kommt
he lives. er her.

ADELAIDE

How well you have described him. I know [4] O wie Sie ihn beschreiben! Das ist er!
him — Elemer. Elemer!
Splendid! Why does he hesitate? [9] Herrlich! — Doch warum zögert er?

FORTUNE-TELLER

It's she who won't consent. Die Zögerung kommt von ihr.

ADELAIDE
(jubilant)

You see through a girl as through a glass — Sie sehen durch die Menschen wie Glas!
it is her unrelenting pride. O Lord, release [5] Das ist ihr namenloser Stolz. O Gott,
her from her pride! erweiche ihren Stolz!
She is as proud as she is lovely. Er ist so gross wie ihre Schönheit.

There is a knock. Zdenka runs to the door.

56

No! I simply can't disturb her.   Nein, jetzt ist es ganz unmöglich!

She is again handed a bill, which she puts with the others.

ADELAIDE

What is it now? Why suddenly this frown?   Was meinen Sie? Was runzeln Sie die Stirn?

FORTUNE-TELLER
(*over her cards*)

I see another man   [10a] Es drängt sich wer hinein
coming between your daughter and the   zwischen die schöne Tochter und den
wealthy one.   reichen Herrn!

ADELAIDE

Holy Lord in Heaven, say, it shall not be!   [3] Heil'ge Mutter Gottes, lass es nicht
                                                                    gescheh'n!
[10a]

FORTUNE-TELLER

What? Do you mean to tell me there's   Wie? Haben Euer Gnaden eine zweite
another daughter?   Tochter?
Oh! That could be a very serious threat!   [6] O das wird eine ernstliche Gefahr!

ADELAIDE
(*kneeling*)

You angels in your Heaven — hear the   [3] Ihr Engelscharen droben, hört das Flehen
prayers of a mother   einer Mutter
whose heart cries out to you!   in ihrer Herzensangst!

ZDENKA
(*frightened*)

Mama!   [10a] Mama!

ADELAIDE

Zdenka, be still! And don't pay any heed to [10b] Zdenka, bleib still und kümmere dich um
what she says.   nichts, was hier geschieht!
                    (*pointing to Zdenka*)
This is . . . my daughter.   [10b] Leise, sie ist es!

FORTUNE-TELLER

Not that youngster there?   Dort der junge Herr?

ADELAIDE

That is my daughter. She was wilder than a [10b] Sie ist ein Mädchen. Weil sie wild war wie
boy,   ein Bub,
and so we let her always be a boy in trousers.   hat man sie weiterhin als Buben laufen
                    lassen.
We are not rich enough to bring up   [3] Wir sind nicht reich genug, in dieser Stadt
two young ladies as it would befit our   zwei Mädchen standeswürdig
station.   auszuführen —
And yet, the girl is fond of her sister —   [10b] allein sie liebt die ältere Schwester über
loves her with devotion.   alle Massen;
She'd never want to do her harm.   [10a] wie könnte sie ihr Böses tun?

FORTUNE-TELLER

The cards are always true.   Die Karten lügen nicht.
The soldier over here — and there the girl [6] Da steht der Offizier. Da steht das blonde
with blond hair.   [10b] Mädchen.
I see two flashing sabres . . . and the fiancé [6] Gezogne Säbel seh ich, und der
seems to withdraw.   Bräutigam zieht sich zurück.
At least you have been warned.   Die Karten warnen Sie!

ADELAIDE
(getting up)

Let's go to my room. There we'll do the whole thing over.	[3]	Hier in mein Zimmer! Sie versuchen es noch einmal!

She leads the fortune-teller into the other room.

ZDENKA
(taking a look at all the bills that lie on the table)

That's quite a lot of bills! They even say they'll sue us.   Sie wollen alle Geld! Sie droh'n mit den Gerichten!

What? No-one told me about this. It says here   Was? davon weiss ich ja gar nichts: sie schreiben:

there are rumours that we are about to leave the city!   [6]   Sie haben schon gehört, dass wir verreisen wollen!

Oh! Everything is lost —   [11]   O! dann ist alles aus!

then I'll not see him again!   [12]   Dann seh ich ihn nie mehr!

Frightened, she runs to the door to listen.

She says . . . that Arabella must look out . . . [10a] Sie sagt: der Arabella droht etwas — an officer she sees . . .   von einem Offizier.

'He won't come here again' answers Mama, 'My child is much too good for him.'   Er darf nicht mehr ins Haus, sagt die Mama, sie wird kompromittiert von ihm.

Not come again? Oh, Lord, I'm sure he'll [12] Nicht mehr ins Haus? O Gott — dann take his life —   bringt er sich ja um —

and that means it will be known he did it for her!   und alle wissen darum: es ist wegen ihr —

And she — she, too, will know it — how [5] und sie — dann endlich weiss sie, wie er sie much he has loved her.   [10a]   geliebt hat!

She moves away from the door.

Dear Lord, this must not be! Please do not make us travel.   Mein Gott, lass das nicht zu, dass wir verreisen müssen!

Make my Papa the winner . . . or perhaps . . . my aunt might die soon?   Lass den Papa gewinnen! Lass in Görz die Tante sterben!

Make Arabella love Matteo more than [10a] Mach, dass die Bella den Matteo über alles anything —   liebt,

make him a happy man, and make us very wealthy.   und dass er glücklich wird, und dass wir nicht mehr arm sind!

I'll sacrifice myself in return, and all my life   Aufopfern will ich mich dafür — mein Leben lang

I'll run around in trousers and renounce, yes, gladly renounce the world!   in Bubenkleidern laufen und Verzicht auf alles, auf alles tun!

Somebody knocks. Matteo enters, opening the door very cautiously. He is in uniform, but without sabre, and cap in hand. Zdenka goes pale. [10a]

Matteo!   Matteo!

MATTEO

Zdenko! You? Are you alone?   [6]   Zdenko! Du! Bist du allein?

ZDENKA
(in a low voice, afraid)

My mother is in there.   Da drin ist die Mama.

MATTEO

And Arabella?   [5] Und Arabella?

ZDENKA

She has gone out to take a walk with her companion.   Sie ist spazieren auf dem Ring mit der Begleiterin.

MATTEO
(one step closer)

No word for me? No word? No note? [12, 6] Und nichts für mich? Kein Wort? Kein Brief?

Zdenka shakes her head sadly. [13]

58

| What happened last night? | Und gestern abend? |

ZDENKA

| She went to the opera, with our Mama. | War sie in der Oper, Mit der Mama. |

MATTEO
(jealous)

| With your Mama alone? | [6] Mit der Mama allein? |

ZDENKA
(hesitating)

| It seems that our three Counts were of the party. | Ich glaub mit der Mama und den drei Grafen. |

MATTEO

| This afternoon? | Und Nachmittag? |

ZDENKA
(hesitating, anxiously)

| They said they would call for my sister and me — for a sleigh-ride. | Sie kommen mit Schlitten und holen sie [9 part] ab — ich soll auch mit. |

MATTEO
(deeply struck)

| To this it had to come between the two of us! Yes! Without you I should not even know what she does. | [13, 6, 12] Dahin ist es gekommen zwischen mir und ihr! Hätt' ich nicht dich — Ich wüsst nicht einmal mehr, was sie tut! |

| As a chaperon they take me along. | Ein Chaperon muss doch auch dabei sein. |

MATTEO

| I am nothing to her, and all I get is, now and then, an absent-minded glance. | Sie hat nichts mehr für mich, als hie und da [5] einen halb finstern, halb zerstreuten Blick! |

ZDENKA

| And yet she's fond of you. Really! I know it. | [11] Und doch hat sie dich lieb! Glaub mir! Ich weiss es. |

MATTEO
(brightening)

| You do? But has she ever told you? | [13] Du weisst's? Sie hat es dir gestanden? |

ZDENKA

| Did she not write you a letter three days ago? You recall your happiness? | Hat sie dir nicht vor drei Tagen [10a] den Brief geschrieben, über den du selig warst? |

MATTEO [6, 12]

| Oh, three-times happy! Oh, that letter was heaven-sent! But then again she seems so cold, a stranger to my heart. How can I ever grasp it — and how bear it, Zdenko — how? | O dreimal selig — wie vom Himmel war der Brief! [13] Dann aber geht sie wieder kalt und fremd an mir vorbei! Wie soll ich das begreifen und ertragen Zdenko — wie? |

ZDENKA
(softly, momentously)

| That's how a girl is — wanting to surrender more and more, | [10b] So ist ein Mädel. Geben will ein Mädel mehr und mehr — |

59

yet never showing it. She's much too much ashamed!	[10a] nur zeigen will sie nichts. Sie schämt sich halt so furchtbar.

MATTEO

You understand, my dearest boy,	Wie du das weisst, du lieber Bub!
and so you also know —	So weisst du auch —

He touches Zdenka's arm but she shakes him off.

what hours I must live through,	[12] was das für Stunden sind
and what bitter thoughts gain power over me,	[13, 6] und was für Gedanken da Herrschaft haben über mich,
when she seems to look through me as through empty air,	wenn sie so durch mich durchschaut wie durch leere Luft —
and when you do not bring to me	und du mir nicht ein Zeichen bringst,
a token that can give me hope of living!	von dem ich wieder hoffen kann und leben!

ZDENKA
(hastily)

I know. But you will get a letter again soo	[10a] Gewiss. Ich bring dir wieder solch' einen Brief —
Yes — tomorrow.	heut oder morgen!

MATTEO

No, today! You are my only friend;	Heute noch! Du bist mein einziger Freund!
give me your word on it — I always trust in you!	Gib mir dein Manneswort — auf dich verlass ich mich!
And if I should no longer feel that I could trust you,	Und wenn ich mich auf dich nicht mehr verlassen könnte,
then something else would happen!	Dann käme etwas andres!

ZDENKA
(full of fear)

What would happen then, Matteo?	Was? was käme dann, Matteo?

MATTEO
(very darkly)

Tomorrow, when they call the roll, I should request a transfer to Galicia.	Dann stünd ich morgen beim Rapport und bäte um Versetzung nach Galizien,
If that, too, does not help,	und wenn mir das nichts hilft und ich auch dort
and if I can't forget my Arabella even there, [5]	die Arabella nicht vergessen kann,
then there's no other way out — but the revolver!	dann gibt's halt einen Ausweg: den Revolver.

ZDENKA

Good Lord in Heaven!	[10a] Mein Gott im Himmel!

MATTEO

Better think how you can help!	Denk daran, wie du mir hilfst!

He leaves hastily.

ZDENKA
(almost beside herself with excitement and fear)

How can I? Oh, my Lord! Help him! And who helps me?	Ihm helfen — o mein Gott! Und mir! Wer hilft denn mir!
It's not so hard to find the words for hundreds of such letters,	[11] Die Wörter hätt' ich wohl in mir für hundert solche Briefe,
and I can forge her writing in my sleep —	und auch die Schrift, die treff' ich ja im Schlaf;
but what's the use of tender words	was aber hilft ihm denn ein Brief, wenn ich für sie
if it is I who's writing them, instead of Arabella!	die zärtlichen verliebten Wörter schreibe! —
The words that I must find are words to [12, 5] touch *her* heart,	Die Wörter muss ich finden, die ins Herz ihr gehn,

60

to make her see the only one who may deserve to be adored by her!
That is more difficult . . . and if I don't [6] succeed, then all is lost.

dass sie erkennt den Einzigen, der es verdient, von ihr geliebt zu sein —
Das ist das Schwerere, und wenn's mir nicht gelingt — hab ich verspielt.

Arabella enters, wearing a fur coat and a hat, followed by her companion. [14]

ARABELLA

I thank you, Fräulein. Please call tomorrow at the same time as today.
Now I don't need you any more. Adieu.

Ich danke, Fräulein. Holen Sie mich morgen um die gleiche Zeit,
für heute brauch' ich Sie nicht mehr. Adieu.

The companion leaves. Arabella sees the roses on a small table.

Those lovely roses! Brought here by a [4, 8] black hussar?

Die schönen Rosen! Hat die ein Husar gebracht?

She lifts the roses out of their vase.

ZDENKA

Why a hussar?

Wie? Ein Husar?

ARABELLA

The adjutant of someone who's a stranger here . . .

Der Leibhusar von einem fremden Reisenden!

ZDENKA

No. They are from Matteo. [13]

Nein, sie sind von Matteo.

Arabella hastily puts the roses down. Zdenka arranges them again in the vase. Tenderly:

Is that how you treat a gift from him? [15]
And yet he sends you new ones every day. [4]

So gehst du mit seinen Blumen um!
Und trotzdem bringt er neue jeden Tag.

ARABELLA
(shortly)

Enough! Who brought those other flowers there?

Ah, lass! — Und dort das andere Bukett?

ZDENKA

Count Elemer.
And this perfume from Dominik, and lace from Lamoral.

Vom Elemer.
Und der Parfüm vom Dominik, und Spitzen vom Lamoral.

ARABELLA
(scornfully)

Those three are spending all they have — [13]
all three are set to win the same beloved.[9part]
I see it come that in the end all three propose to me!

Die drei! Verlumpen Geld zu dritt, verlieben sich zu dritt ins gleiche Mädel —
am End verloben sie sich auch noch alle drei mit mir!

ZDENKA

Unworthy three! And yet there is only one [15] who's worthy — it's . . .

Nichts wert sind sie — und etwas wert ist nur der eine, der!

She holds Matteo's roses out to her.

ARABELLA

Ah, don't! Those three are funnier!

Ah, lass! Die drei sind lustiger.

ZDENKA
(reproachfully)

How can you say that!
It's he who loves you with his heart's [15, 16] devotion!

Kannst du das sagen!
Er liebt dich doch aus seiner ganzen Seele, —

ARABELLA
(scornfully)

. . . and with everything that's in him. [12]

— und aus allen seinen Kräften.

61

ZDENKA
(violently)

You once were fond of him.

Du hast ihn lieb gehabt!

ARABELLA

Perhaps I was. [5]
But that is past; that's what you said!

Vielleicht!
Gehabt! So ist's vorbei: du sagst es selbst.

ZDENKA

Be sure not to say that ever to him, [12, 10a]
(violently)
for he would die. You are his one and all.

Gib acht, dass er dich das aussprechen hört!
Es wär' sein Tod! Anbeten tut er dich!

ARABELLA
(watching her closely)

Zdenkerl — the way you talk in that [3, 10a]
excited tone — just like Mama!
Be on your guard!

Zdenkerl, du hast schon ganz den
exaltierten Ton von der Mama!
Pass auf auf dich.

ZDENKA
(passionately)

It almost breaks my heart when I must see [15]
his grief.

Weil's mir das Herz umdreht, wenn ich ihn
leiden seh'!

ARABELLA
(without looking at her)

Are you in love with him?

Bist du verliebt in ihn?

ZDENKA

I am his friend —
his only friend in all this world!

Sein Freund bin ich!
Sein einziger Freund auf dieser Welt!

ARABELLA
(looking at her searchingly again)

Zdenkerl, I feel there's something [13]
dangerous in you these days!
It might be time you were a girl once more, [10a]

for all the world, and that this masquerade
were ended.

Zdenkerl, in dir steckt was Gefährliches
seit letzter Zeit.
Mir scheint, Zeit wär's, dass du ein Mädel
wirst
vor aller Welt und die Maskerad' ein End'
hat.

ZDENKA

I'll be a boy until I die. I'll never be a [15, 6]
woman, [17]
not a woman like you: proud, a coquette, [5]
and cold of heart.

Ich bleib ein Bub bis an mein End. Ich will
nicht eine Frau sein —
so wie du eine bist. Stolz und kokett und
kalt dabei!

ARABELLA
(very seriously) [13]

He's not the one who's right for me.

Er ist der Richtige nicht für mich!

Arabella sits. Zdenka makes an abrupt movement.

I'm serious now. I only tell you what is [17]
true. [4]
It's really not my fault — that's how I am! [14]
A man may soon mean much to me,
but suddenly, he means no longer anything. [13]

It happens right in here, and soon — I [5]
don't know how —
something begins to ask, and I — I do not
know
what the answer is! I try by day and night,

Ich red' im Ernst, ich red' die Wahrheit jetzt
zu dir!
Ich kann ja nichts dafür, dass ich so bin.
Ein Mann wird mir gar schnell recht viel
und wieder schnell ist er schon gar nichts
mehr für mich!
Da drin im Kopf geschieht's und schnell, ich
weiss nicht wie!
Es fängt zu fragen an, und auf die Fragen
find' ich die Antwort nicht, bei Tag und
nicht bei Nacht.

and, quite without my will, my heart begins to turn, it turns away from him. It's really not my fault. The one who's right for me, if there is one [7] for me in all this world, he will stand before me, all at once, his eyes upon me, mine on him, and no more doubting will remain, and no more asking. And happy, so happy I shall be, and obedient like a child.

[17] Ganz ohne meinen Willen dreht sich dann mein Herz und dreht sich los von ihm. Ich kann ja nichts dafür — aber der Richtige — wenn's einen gibt für mich auf dieser Welt — der wird einmal dastehn, da vor mir, und wird mich anschaun und ich ihn, und keine Zweifel werden sein und keine Fragen. und selig werd' ich sein und gehorsam wie ein Kind.

ZDENKA
(after a short silence, looking at her lovingly)

I do not know your heart — you may be right or wrong — but I am much too fond of you to know. I want you to be happy with someone who is worthy. And let me give my help to you.

Ich weiss nicht, wie du bist, ich weiss nicht, ob du Recht hast — dazu hab' ich dich viel zu lieb! Ich will nur, dass du glücklich wirst mit einem, der's verdient! und helfen will ich dir dazu.

(still tenderly, more to herself)

For this is what the fortune-teller said: 'She bathed in light, and I in utter darkness . . .'

So hat ja die Prophetin es gesehn sie ganz im Licht, und ich hinab ins Dunkel.

(aside)

She is so lovely and so sweet. I'll go away,

and still in parting I will bless you, yes I will bless you, dearest sister.

Sie ist so schön und so lieb — ich werde gehn,
und noch im Gehn werd' ich dich segnen, meine Schwester.

ARABELLA
(to herself, with Zdenka)

The one who's right for me, if there is one [7, 8] for me in all this world, he will stand before me, all at once, his eyes upon me, mine on him, and no more doubting will remain, and no more asking. And happy, so happy I shall be, and obedient like a child.

Aber der Richtige, wenn's einen gibt für mich auf dieser Welt, der wird einmal dastehn, da vor mir und wird mich anschaun, und ich ihn, und keine Zweifel werden sein und keine Fragen. und selig werd' ich sein und gehorsam wie ein Kind!

Sleigh-bells are heard in the distance.

ZDENKA

That is the sleigh of Count Elemer — I know those jingles.

Das ist der Schlitten vom Elemer. Ich kenn' die Schellen.

ARABELLA
(gay again)

And Dominik, I am sure, is right behind him, and after him, Count Lamoral; that's how [13] they carry on. And I? I go along because today is Carnival! [14]

Und hinter ihm kommt der Dominik gefahren, und hinter dem der Lamoral. So treiben sie's, und ich — ich treib' halt mit — weil halt nur einmal Fasching ist.

ZDENKA

No! It is only Elemer today. Are you glad? No! He's not the one who's right for you!

Nein: heute kommt der Elemer allein. Freust du dich? Nein! Er kann der Richtige nicht sein!

I do not know. Perhaps . . . I have to take [13] Ich weiss ja nicht! — Kann sein, ich muss
him.   ihn nehmen.

She is thoughtful.

ZDENKA

No, no, that must not be!   Nein, nein, das darf nicht sein!

ARABELLA
(*to herself, paying no attention to Zdenka*)

This evening ends the Carnival, and this   Heut abend ist der Fasching aus. Heut
evening I must give my answer.   abend muss ich mich entscheiden.

ZDENKA

Oh, Lord! Matteo will destroy himself! [6, 10a] Oh Gott, dann bringt sich der Matteo um —
(*as though she sees a vision*)
I'm knocking at his door . . . he does not   Ich klopf' an seine Tür, es gibt nicht
answer . . .   Antwort,
I hug his lifeless form, and kiss his icy lips, ich werf' mich über ihn — ich küss zum
                                                            ersten Mal
for the first and the last time! Everything   seine eiskalten Lippen! Dann ist alles aus.
is lost!

ARABELLA
(*at the window*)

Zdenka, there was a stranger here, not long [7, 8] Siehst du, da war ein fremder Mensch heut
ago,   vormittag,
just as I left the house to take my walk.   wie ich hier aus dem Haus gegangen bin,
I saw him stand there, at the corner, tall, he dort drüben war er an der Ecke, gross, in
wore a heavy fur.   einem Reisepelz,
And right behind, his ow.. hussar. From   Und hinter ihm ein Leibhusar — ein
out of town.   Fremder halt
Hungarian? Or perhaps from somewhere   aus Ungarn oder aus der Wallachei . . .
else.
And as he looked at me, with eyes so big [17] der hat mich angeschaut mit grossen,
and grave and earnest,   ernsten, festen Augen.
I could have sworn an oath I would find   Ich hätt' geschworen drauf, dass er mir
flowers here,   Blumen schickt.
flowers from him! That gift would mean [4] Blumen von dem, das wäre heute mehr für
much more than any other.   mich als alles.

ZDENKA
(*tearing Matteo's roses out of the vase and holding them up to Arabella*)

Take these! They come from one who's [12] Nimm die! Sie kommen von dem treusten
true and faithful like no other.   Menschen auf der Welt.
Hold them quite close — quite close to you   Nimm sie zu dir, ganz nah zu dir, nimm
— don't take any others than these!   keine anderen als die!
I feel — my and your fate depend on it!   Ich fühl's: dein und mein Schicksal hängt
                                                            daran!

The sound of sleigh-bells comes nearer.

ARABELLA
(*astonished*)

What's wrong with you? You are so strange [9] Was hast du denn? was ist denn los mit dir?
today.

ZDENKA

Be still — there comes Count Elemer.   Sei still! Da kommt der Elemer.

*She leaves quickly. Count Elemer stands in the doorway. He takes off the fur which was
hanging over his shoulders and throws it to Zdenka who closes the door behind her. [9]*

ARABELLA

You're strutting like a victor on the march! | So triumphierend treten Sie herein?

ELEMER

This is my day! We have been drawing lots,
and I have brought the finest of my horses.
Today I'm the one who takes you for a
  sleigh-ride,
and later on, down at the Coachman's
  Ball,
I'll be your master!

Heut ist mein Tag! So haben wir gelost.
Anspannen lassen hab' ich meine Russen,
denn heut darf ich Sie in meinem Schlitten
  führen,
und abends dann auf dem Fiakerball
[5] bin ich Ihr Herr!

Arabella frowns.

I mean, I'll be your favourite slave,
for you must always be the reigning
  Queen!

Ich meine: ich Ihr erster Knecht,
[19] denn Sie sind immerdar die Königin!

ARABELLA

You have been drawing lots? Incorrigible
  rascals!

[13] Ihr habt um mich gelost! Ihr seid mir schon
  die Rechten!

ELEMER

Yes! One among us three it has to be whom
  you must favour.
That was decided, and we took an oath on
  it.

Ja, einer von uns dreien muss es sein, den
  sie erwählen!
So ist's beschlossen und beschworen unter
  uns.

ARABELLA

Ah! One among you three it has to be?
And I? I am a slave girl, and my fate has
  been revealed by drawing lots!
But in what war have I become your booty,
  if I may inquire?

Ah! einer von euch dreien muss es sein?
Und ich? Ich bin die Sklavin, über die ihr
  schon das Los geworfen habt?
In welchem Krieg habt ihr mich denn
  erbeutet, wenn ich fragen darf?

ELEMER

What war? But it was you who named the
  prize,
and with your glances you defied the three
  of us to fight!
A girl can talk with eyes. They give — they
  take —
And they bespeak still more!

Zum Preis hat sie sich selber eingesetzt,
mit ihren Blicken hat sie uns gefordert, ihr
  zu stehn,
[20] ein Mädchenblick ist stark und gibt und
  nimmt —
und er verheisst noch mehr!

ARABELLA

Is that the truth? I should be furious then
  with you
that you have paid me court all through
  the Carnival,
and still no-one has ever unchained my
  heart,
and I am still the same I always was before.

[7] Verheisst er das? Dann sollt' ich zornig
  sein auf euch,
dass ihr mir jetzt den Hof macht einen
  Fasching lang,
und immer noch habt ihr mir nicht das
  Herz erlöst,
und immer bin ich noch die gleiche, die ich
  war,

And this one happiness — so bitter and so
  sweet —
that's left to any girl, I'm tasting now . . .
  to hide . . .
suspended in the air . . . and never quite
  abandoned . . .
and wavering still . . . and still . . .
perhaps . . . could be that very soon there
  may be coming something else!

und dieses einzige bittersüsse Glück,
das einem Mädel bleibt, das kost' ich aus:
  versteckt
und in der Schwebe sein und keinem ganz
  sich geben!
und zögern noch und noch —
[17] Vielleicht, — vielleicht wird aber bald was
  andres kommen Elemer.

(with a sweet smile)

Who knows? Perhaps . . . quite soon . . .
  perhaps this very night!

Wer weiss — vielleicht sehr bald, vielleicht
  noch diese Nacht!

65

This something will happen at the moment [19]
for which
I've often prayed to Heaven, Bella,
when you throw over all those lily-livered
hesitations [5]
and dare to be what you are — the loveliest
of all,
and meant to shower happiness on only me
alone, and no-one else!
Do you hear the horses? How they're
stamping,
and how their jingles tinkle? They are
saying:
'You want to! Come!' We'll fly together
down the roads.
Thought is the end of life, and happy those
who never think!

Das andere wird kommen in der Stunde,
die ich herab vom Himmel flehe, Bella —
wo Sie abwerfen diese feigen, zaudernden
Bedenken
und das sein wollen, was Sie sind, das
herrlichste Geschöpf,
geschaffen, Seligkeit zu bringen. Über
mich allein auf dieser Welt!
Hören Sie meine Pferde? Wie sie stampfen

und ihre Glocken schütteln? Wie sie läuten:

du willst ja! Komm! dann sausen wir mit
dir dahin!
Nachdenken ist der Tod: im Nicht-
bedenken liegt das Glück!

ARABELLA

Are those your horses? Shaking their
manes so impatiently?
I want to go! Today is Mardi Gras,

and today when midnight strikes, the
Carnival ends.
We'll flit along the main road till it takes
my breath away!
My brother Zdenko comes along. [13]

Sind es die Russen? Schütteln sie sich
schon vor Ungeduld?
Ja, ja, ich will. Heut ist doch Faschings-
dienstag,
und heut um Mitternacht ist alles aus.

Die Hauptallee hinunter — dass der Atem
mir vergeht
— aber der Zdenko fahrt mit uns.

ELEMER
(furious, unhappy)

No word? No word?
I may not say a word to you then?

Kein Wort, kein Wort
soll ich zu Ihnen reden dürfen?

ARABELLA

In less than thirty minutes I'll be downstairs
with him. Your horses will have to be
patient a short while.

In einer halben Stunde bin ich unten
mit ihm. Solange müssen sich die Russen
gedulden!

(quite decided, dismissing him)

He comes along! Auf Wiedersehen!

Der Bub kommt mit! Auf Wiedersehen!

ELEMER

You are cruel! You are the most enchanting
girl on earth —
incomprehensible — and heartless — and
the one whom I adore!

Sie sind ein angebetetes Geschöpf, Sie
Grausame!
ein unbegreifliches! ein grausames!
entzückendes Geschöpf.

He leaves.

ZDENKA
(coming back)

Did you get rid of him?

Hast du ihn fortgeschickt?

ARABELLA

We'll take a ride with him. Go and get
dressed.
A sleigh-ride.

Wir fahren aus mit ihm. Schnell, zieh dich
an!
Im Schlitten.

ZDENKA

Must I come along?

Dazu brauchst du mich?

ARABELLA

Yes, you must come along.
The sleigh-bells sound still louder.

Ja, dazu brauch ich dich.

Look there! The fiery horses — how they prance and shake their manes . . .	Schau doch die schönen Rappen, wie sie ungeduldig sind.

(in a suddenly changed tone)

Zdenka!	Zdenka!

ZDENKA

What is it? What has frightened you?	Was ist denn? was erschrickst du so?

ARABELLA

He! I see him! My stranger! There, across [18] the street there!	Er! das ist er! mein Fremder! da! dort drüben geht er
And that's his servant. I am sure he's searching where my house is. [17]	mit seinem Diener. Sicher will er wissen, wo ich wohne.
You see, he tries to find out where my windows are.	Pass auf, jetzt sucht er, welches meine Fenster sind.
Look at those eyes of his! How big they are! What grave and earnest eyes!	Schau seine Augen an, was das für grosse ernste Augen sind.

ZDENKA

(behind her)

I don't know what his eyes are like; he never once looked up.	Wie soll ich seine Augen seh'n, er schaut ja nicht herauf.

ARABELLA

No, he does not look up.	[7] Nein, er schaut nicht herauf.

She turns back into the room.

A passing stranger.	Er geht vorüber.

ZDENKA

You want to ride out with Count Elemer?	So willst du fahren mit dem Elemer?

ARABELLA

Of course. Go, and hurry up. You come along. Get dressed.	Ja, ja. Geh' und zieh' dich an. Du fahrst mit uns. Ich will's.

ZDENKA

Psst . . . that's Mama!	Pst, die Mama.

Adelaide has entered, listening: she has heard Waldner coming in. He appears at the door, well-dressed in fur coat, high hat, with cane and gloves. He is elegant but looks somewhat the worse for lack of sleep; he crosses the room, without seeing anything, and sinks into an armchair downstage right.

ADELAIDE [3]

Leave us alone, you and Zdenka. Your papa has his worries.	Lasst uns allein, meine Kinder, [1] euer Vater hat Sorgen.

Arabella and Zdenka leave at opposite sides of the stage.

WALDNER

He stands up, takes off his coat — behind a screen — and puts his hat on the table. He sees the envelopes with all the bills in them and mechanically starts opening them one after another.

Is that the whole mail? No-one writes to us anymore.	Nichts als das Zeug da? und von niemand sonst ein Brief?

ADELAIDE

You've played again, and lost our money, Theodor?	Du hast gespielt? Du hast verloren, Theodor?

Waldner is silent.

I thought you'd written to some comrades you knew in the army?	Du hast an deine Regimentskameraden geschrieben?

WALDNER

Not one has even answered! That is sad.	Von keinem eine Antwort, das ist hart.

He throws himself into the easy chair: half to Adelaide, half to himself:

I once knew a certain Mandryka;	Da war ein gewisser Mandryka,
he was wealthy and full of strange ideas.	der war steinreich und ein Phantast dazu.
For a girl whom he courted he once ordered all the streets of Verona	Für ein Mädel hat der einmal die Strassen von Verona
covered with three thousand buckets of salt	bestreuen lassen mit dreitausend Scheffeln Salz,
because she felt like going on a sleigh-ride in July!	weil sie hat Schlitten fahren wollen mitten im August!
I asked him to be generous to a friend, [4]	Ich hab' an seine Grossmut appelliert —
and I sent a picture of Bella with my note,	und hab' von der Bella ein Bild hineingelegt —
in her grey and blue ball-dress, with marabou trim. [5]	in dem stahlblauen Ballkleid mit Schwanenbesatz —
I said to myself: who knows? Maybe he'll come	Ich hab' mir gedacht: vielleicht kommt er daher,
and, fool that he is, he'll offer her marriage.	ein Narr, wie er ist, und heirat' das Mädel!

ADELAIDE

You mean our child should marry one as old as you?	O Gott, mein schönes Kind mit einem alten Mann!

WALDNER
(violently)

It's time that we found one who's sure to propose,	Es muss ein solider Bewerber daher
and an end must be made to this flirting [7] about,	und ein End mit der ewigen Hofmacherei,
which is useless.	die zu nichts führt!

(walking up and down restlessly)

Otherwise, there's no way out!	Ich weiss sonst keinen Ausweg!

ADELAIDE
(suddenly carried away)

Let's be gone to Aunt Jadwiga!	Fort mit uns! Zur Tante Jadwiga,
She will receive us in her castles!	Sie nimmt uns auf, auf ihre Schlösser!
You'll be her steward.	Du wirst Verwalter,
I'll do my share, keeping house.	ich führe der Tante das Haus!

WALDNER

And your daughters?	Und die Mädeln?

ADELAIDE

Zdenka remains a boy for ever.	Zdenka wird Groom für ew'ge Zeiten —
In our sad condition	wir sind nicht in der Lage,
two daughters are too many!	zwei Töchter zu erhalten!
And Arabella — the cards foretold her luck —	Und Arabella — ihr ist prophezeit,
she will be saved by an outstanding marriage! [19]	sie macht ihr Glück durch eine grosse Heirat!

WALDNER
(grimly)

And meantime we'll have spent our last ten gulden bill.	Inzwischen ist der letzte Fünfziger dahin!

ADELAIDE

Don't worry, Theodor, I dreamed last night —	Sie ruhig, Theodor, mir sind im Traum drei Nummern erschienen!
I dreamt of three numbers — infallible, exquisite numbers!	Unfehlbare, herrliche Zahlen!

WALDNER

Foolish talk!	Ah, Geschwätz!

Go, pawn your old pearl brooch, and give me the cash.
What? But where is the brooch? It's gone! You've pawned it?

Versetz die Smaragdbrosch' und gib mir das Geld!
Was, du hast sie nicht mehr? Versetzt? Verpfändeṭ?

ADELAIDE

Yes, last week I pawned it. We've no more jewels.

Schon vorige Woche. Sie war das Letzte.

WALDNER

Today would be my day!
I would be in luck!
I feel it in my fingers!

[1, 2, 3] Und heut hätt' ich Glück!
Ich spür's in jedem Finger!
Du unglückselige Person!

ADELAIDE

Oh, curse this Vienna!
And yet, I often dreamt this dream:
from deep despair Vienna will lift us up

to highest summits — by the hand of beauty!

O dieses Wien!
Allein, so hab' ich's oft geträumt!
Aus tiefster Schmach hebt's uns einmal empor
zu höchster Höhe durch die Hand der Schönheit!

WALDNER

My poor and self-deluded wife! I have not even one gulden to my name.

Ich hab' nicht einen Gulden mehr im Sack!

ADELAIDE
(*still dreaming she withdraws; on the point of leaving*)

Don't you recall that even dukes and princes
once in a while are known to make a love-match?

Hat's denn vielleicht im Allerhöchsten Erzhaus
noch keine Liebesheiraten gegeben?

She leaves quickly.

WALDNER
(*reading his bills*)

. . . 'regret to inform you' . . . 'can wait no longer' . . .
. . . 'just a last reminder' . . . 'shall have to sue you' . . .
My poor wife! My poor daughters!

'Bin nicht in der Lage, länger zu warten!'

'Müsste die Gerichte in Anspruch nehmen.'

[8] Arme Frau! Arme Mädeln!

He rings for a waiter and a waiter appears.

Cognac!

Cognac!

WAITER

I have orders not to serve Number 8

any more — except against cash.

Auf Nummer 8 darf ich nichts mehr servieren!
Ausser wünschen sofort zu bezahlen!

WALDNER

That is enough! I'll do without.

Verschwinden Sie. Ich brauche nichts.

The waiter leaves.

This moment . . . they sit down . . . and start another round of gambling!
When I'm not gambling, that is so much time lost.

Jetzt setzen sie sich hin und fangen wieder an zu spielen.
[1, 8] Und alles andre ist verlorene Zeit!

WAITER
(*returning with a tray*)

A gentleman to see you.

Ein Herr!

WALDNER

Just tell him I am not at home now.
Put it down there.

Sie sagen, ich bin ausgegangen.
Das Zeug dorthin!

The waiter puts a visiting card on the table and leaves.

But this is not a bill? What is it?	Das ist ja keine Rechnung.
I've never heard yet that creditors first present their card!	Melden sich die Lieferanten jetzt schon mit Visitenkarten an?

He goes to the table, picks up the card and is pleasantly surprised.

Mandryka!	Mandryka!
That wealthy fellow, my dear old friend [4] from army days.	Der reiche Kerl! Mein bester Freund im Regiment!

WAITER
(at the door again)

The gentleman insists ...	Der Herr fragt dringend an.

WALDNER

He's more than welcome! [5, 14]	Ich lasse bitten!

(welcoming his visitor with open arms) [18]

Friend, I am glad ...	Tschau, Kamerad!

Mandryka enters; a tall, elegant man, not more than thirty-five years old. He is well-dressed, without any provincial extravagance, and yet his whole appearance has a slight rustic tinge. Welko enters behind Mandryka and remains standing by the door. Waldner, flabbergasted, shrinks back.

MANDRYKA

Have I the honour ... are you not Captain Count Waldner?	Hab' ich die Ehre mit dem Rittmeister Graf Waldner?

WALDNER

Waldner, precisely, but Captain no more.	Waldner, so heiss ich, Rittmeister nicht mehr.

Mandryka reaches behind him. Welko hands him a letter, bowing. He takes the letter and walks over to Waldner.

MANDRYKA

Then you must be the writer of this letter?	Sind Sie, Herr Graf, der Schreiber dieses Briefes?

Waldner takes the letter which is creased and much blood-stained. Mandryka continues very casually, both briskly and courteously.

You see, there are some bloodstains on it that make it hard to read.	Er ist ein biss'l blutig worden und nicht mehr leserlich.
The very day when they brought me the letter I was out hunting,	Ich bin den Tag, wo er mir zugekommen,
chasing a she-bear. She took me on for battle	auf eine alte Bärin gegangen, sie hat mich angenommen
and she scratched me a bit. That's how it came about.	und ein biss'l gekratzt — dabei ist das passiert.

WALDNER
He has taken one glance at the letter and returns it.

I wrote a letter, that is true, to someone who is your namesake.	Geschrieben hab' ich allerdings an einen Herrn Ihres Namens —
He was my friend, and also my brother-in-arms.	er war mein Freund und Regiments-kamerad.

MANDRYKA

That was my uncle. He is dead, and I am [7] now the last Mandryka.	Das war mein Onkel. Er ist tot. Ich bin der einzige Mandryka.
I hope you will forgive my being bold enough to read	Somit verzeihen Sie, dass ich den Brief
your note you sent. Now — now all must depend on this!	zu öffnen mir gestattete. — Jetzt kommt es auf eines an:
Welko, the picture!	Welko, das Bild!

WELKO
(handing him a photograph and speaking)

Everything is all right, Gospodar.
The beautiful girl with the face lives here.

Es ist in Ordnung, Gospodar.
Das schöne Fräulein mit dem Gesicht
wohnt hier.

MANDRYKA
(with the photograph in his hand) [7, 21]

Dear Count, the letter which I'm holding
here,
which you addressed to him, to my dear
uncle, from friend to friend —
when I received it, a lady's picture was
enclosed.

Herr Graf, Sie haben Ihrem werten Brief,

der kameradschaftlich an meinen Onkel
gerichtet war,
[5] Sie haben dieses Damenbildnis beigelegt.

WALDNER
(hardly looking, not giving it any importance)

That's right, a photograph of my daughter,
Arabella.

Ah ja, die Photographie meiner Tochter
Arabella.

MANDRYKA
(with noticeable agitation but without moving)

And is your daughter unmarried still?

[13] Die gnädige Tochter ist unvermählt — ?

WALDNER
(nodding)

Unmarried still.

Noch unvermählt —

MANDRYKA

... and not engaged as yet?

— und derzeit nicht verlobt?

WALDNER

Not yet engaged.

Derzeit noch nicht.

MANDRYKA
(very earnestly, almost ceremoniously)

If that's the case, will you be good enough
to listen?

Dann bitte ich um ein Gespräch von fünf
Minuten.

*Welko moves two easy-chairs close to each other and retires. Waldner and Mandryka sit
down; a short pause: Mandryka a bit embarrased, Waldner rather anxious.*

May I forget my modesty and ask you just
one question?

[18] Darf ich so unbescheiden sein und eine
Frage stellen?

WALDNER

You are the nephew and heir of one who
was my dearest comrade —
consider me a friend!

Du bist der Neffe — und Erbe meines
teuren Kameraden.
Verfüge über mich!

MANDRYKA

You're very kind.

Ich danke sehr ...

He reflects for a moment.

About your note to my departed uncle ...
when you enclosed this most enchanting
picture,
the picture of your daughter,
am I too forward thinking that you did it —
advertently? I hope you will forgive me.

Als in dem Brief an meinen sel'gen Onkel
das reizende Porträt des Fräulein Tochter
hineingeschlossen wurde,
darf ich annehmen, dass da eine Absicht
im Spiele war? — ich bitte um Vergebung.

WALDNER
(with circumspection)

Good God, I simply told myself,
my dear old Mandryka will ... be amused.

[4] Mein Gott, ich hab' mir halt gedacht,
ich mach' damit dem Alten einen Spass.

71

MANDRYKA
(looking at him very attentively)

You thought he'd be amused? You never [21] Dem Onkel einen Spass? — Wenn aber das
thought that this might well have die Folge wär' gewesen:
happened:
what if my uncle, who was all a man is dass mein Herr Onkel, der ein ganzer
meant to be, Mann gewesen ist
and in the prime of manhood, enchanted [5] und in den besten Jahren, sich hätte in die
by the beauty of this lovely face, Schönheit des Porträts verliebt
had come here, and had stood before you, und wär getreten hier vor Ihnen, hoch-
most respected Count, geborner Herr,
and frankly, as one noble and honest man so als ein offenherziger Edelmann vor
speaks to another, einen andern,
had said to you: 'Whoever sees a face like und hätt' gesagt: wer das Gesicht gesehen
this, hat
and does not woo the girl, is quite unworthy und tritt nicht als Bewerber auf,
to be living on this beautiful earth that verdient nicht, dass ihn Gott auf dieser
God has made — schönen Erde leben lässt:
so give the girl to me, as wife, to reign so gib das Mädel mir zur Frau und Herrin!
above me . . .
and then what would have happened? Was wäre dann gewesen? Gesetzt den Fall,
Let's just assume that's what he should er hätte so gesagt!
have said.

WALDNER

In that case, I fear we should have found Dann hätten wir uns in einer unerwarteten
ourselves in an unforeseen situation! Situation befunden.

MANDRYKA
(standing up, very excited but with self-control)

My uncle is no more. I'm the only Der Onkel ist dahin. Heut bin ich der
Mandryka — no-one else! Mandryka, niemand sonst.
Mine are the forests, mine are all the Mein sind die Wälder, meine sind die
hamlets. Dörfer.
Four thousand subjects pray that I may be Viertausend Untertanen beten, dass ich
a happy man. glücklich sei,
and I, with hands raised high to implore und ich, mit aufgehobenen Händen bitte
you, ich:
pray of you, her father: give to me your [8, 14] Herr Vater, geben mir die gnädige Tochter,
gracious daughter,
do give to me the one who these last fourteen geben Sie mir zur Frau, die jetzt seit
weeks vierzehn Wochen
has reigned as the mistress of every jeden Gedanken in dieser Brust regiert.
thought of mine!
Waldner is amazed and silent. He gestures to Mandryka to sit down again.
Your silence is no condemnation? Ihr Zögern ist kein Todesurteil? Nein!
Waldner shakes his head.
No? You give me hope? Ich darf sie sehen?
Waldner nods. [5]
Consider: I received your note that very Bedenken: dieser Brief kommt an, und in
day, der gleichen Stunde
the very moment this bear decides she nimmt mich die alte Bärin in die Arme
must embrace me,
and hugs me so, four of my ribs are und drückt mir vier von meinen Rippen
smashed! ein.
Twelve weeks I had to lie in bed, disabled, Zwölf Wochen bin ich so im Bett
before my eyes — gelegen —
your daughter's face. One thought Vor meinen Augen dieses Bild — und ein
possessed me, ever stronger, Gedanken immer stärker,
till it had dragged my heart and soul right bis er die Seele mir herausgezogen hat!
out of me . . .
(naively without boasting)
All my stewards come running: 'What Kommen meine Verwalter: was ist's mit
happened to our master?' unserm Herrn?

After them, those who run my dairies: 'What happened to our master?'	Kommen die von den Meierhöfen: was ist's mit unserm Herrn?
After them, those who run my stud-farms: 'Does he not love his horses?'	Kommen die von den Fohlenhöfen: freut unsern Herrn kein Pferd mehr?
After them, my huntsmen: 'Has he abandoned hunting?'	Kommen meine Förster: freut unsern Herrn kein Jagen?
I don't give them any answer. I say 'Welko, [22] go!	Ich geb' ihnen keine Antwort. Welko ruf' ich,
Bring the Jew here, quick! You know, the Jew in Sisek	hol' mir den Juden, na! wie heisst der Jud in Sissek,
who wants to buy my forest. Yes, my oak-wood.	der meinen Wald will kaufen? dort den Eichwald!
Get hold of him; tell him to bring his money.	Schnell her mit ihm, und er soll Geld mitbringen.
Tomorrow morning I will leave, and go to Vienna,	denn morgen fahr' ich in dem Kaiser seine Hauptstadt,
and every breath is so expensive there! [22]	da kostet Geld ein jeder Atemzug,
But nothing must be in my way when I go wooing!'	und Hindernisse darf's nicht geben auf der Brautfahrt!
(*He takes out a large but elegant wallet bulging with thousand gulden notes.*)	
This is my wood!	Das ist der Wald . . .
It was a splendid wood. Hermits were found in it,	Es war ein schöner Wald: Einsiedler waren drin,
and gypsies called it home, and there were roe-bucks . . .	Zigeuner waren drin und alte Hirschen,
and smoke from many kilns was always in the air.	und Kohlenmeiler haben viele drin geraucht —
In one moment, all this turned into shreds of paper.	Hat sich alles in die paar Fetzen Papier verwandelt!
(*with Waldner*)	
But enough sturdy woods of oak trees are standing in my possesssion	Aber es stehen Eichenwälder genug noch auf meinem Boden.
for all of my children — God may grant it!	Für Kinder und Enkel — Gott erhalte!

WALDNER

It's strange to think . . . a wood . . . hermits were found in it . . .	Wenn man bedenkt: ein Wald — Einsiedler waren drin,
and gypsies called it home . . . and there were roe-bucks . . .	Zigeuner waren drin und alte Hirschen,
in a jiffy — there's such a wallet!	und auf eins, zwei — ein solches Porte-feuille!
It has been years since I have seen a thing like that!	Ich hab' seit vielen Jahren so was nicht gesehen!

MANDRYKA

I hope you can forgive me that I talked to you about such matters?	Verzeih'n um Gottes willen, dass ich da von solchen Sachen rede!
It came about . . . I don't know how.	Ist ganz, ich weiss nicht, wie gescheh'n!

Waldner is fascinated by the wallet. Mandryka is about to put it back in his pocket, but Waldner involuntarily stops him.

WALDNER

No, no! It interests me more than you will ever know!	Oho! ich find' es ungeheuer interessant!

MANDRYKA
(*offering him the wallet, with an easy charm*)

May I, perhaps? May I suggest?	Darf ich vielleicht? Brauchst du vielleicht,
A momentary need? I should be much obliged.	So für den Augenblick? Du tust mir eine Gnad'
Take some — I mean it!	[23] Teschek, bedien' dich!

He hesitates a bit but then takes one of the thousand gulden bills.

Yes, my banker's out of town.	Mein Bankier ist nur verreist!
I'll give it back to you not later than tonight.	Ich geb' es dir heut abends spätestens zurück!

MANDRYKA
(offering him the wallet once more)

That's all? Now, don't be bashful — I insist.	Nicht mehr? Ich bitte vielmals! Aber doch!
Take some — I mean it!	[23] Teschek, bedien' dich!

Waldner takes a second note and puts it with the first one in his pocket. Mandryka puts the wallet back in his pocket. — A moment of embarrassment.

When will it be convenient	[7] Und wann wird's dir genehm sein;
to introduce me to your Countess —	mich deiner Gräfin vorzustellen —
and also to your daughter?	und dann der gnädigen Tochter?

WALDNER
(standing up)

They are next door. I think I hear them.	Sie sind gleich da im Nebenzimmer.

Mandryka also stands up.

Let's do it now. Just wait,	Willst du sie sehen? Ich ruf' —
I'll call them in.	ich stell' dich vor.

MANDRYKA

What now? I beg you, no. I'm not prepared.	Jetzt? So? Ich bitte: nein! auf keinen Fall!

WALDNER

Your uncle never was so shy!	So schüchtern war der Onkel nicht!

MANDRYKA
(very earnestly)

But this is quite another case.	[21] Das ist ein Fall von andrer Art.
My feelings are the same as though I were in church.	Es handelt sich für mich um etwas Heiliges.

WALDNER

Just as you say.	Ganz wie du willst!

MANDRYKA
(in a changed tone)

I'll stay right here, and rent my own apartment.	Ich werd' mich hier im Hause einlogieren
I hope you will let me know when your Countess expects	und den Befehl abwarten seiner Gräfin,
to have me call on her. This afternoon?	wann ich mich präsentieren darf am Nachmittag
Or perhaps this evening. I shall await her pleasure.	oder Abend — oder wann es wird belieben.

He bows. Waldner shakes his hand and sees him to the door. [17]

WALDNER
(left alone)

Was this a dream? I think I saw him sit there — right there,	Hab' ich geträumt? Dahier ist er gesessen, dahier,
the nephew of Mandryka.	[22, 23] der Neffe vom Mandryka.
Something like that simply can't be.	So was passiert einem doch nicht!

He takes the two bills out of his pocket; they are a bit crumpled; he carefully smooths them and sneaks them into his empty wallet.

Was it a dream? No, it was *not* a dream!	Hab' ich geträumt? Nein! ich hab' nicht geträumt!

Once again he takes one of the bills out of his pocket and, absent-mindedly, rolls it into a paper cup; then, gaily imitating Mandryka's inflection:

'Take some — I mean it!'	[23] Teschek, bedien' dich!

WAITER
(enters)

You have been ringing?	Ist hier gerufen?

He sees the thousand gulden bill in Waldner's hand and changes his tone.

May I have your orders?	Haben mich befohlen?

WALDNER
(softly and to himself)

'Take some — I mean it!'	[23] Teschek, bedien' dich!

WAITER

You'd like to have this changed to something smaller?	Befehlen diesen Tausender zu wechseln?

WALDNER

Later, perhaps, not now!	Später vielleicht, jetzt nicht.

The waiter leaves.

WALDNER
(to himself, cheerfully)

'Take some — I mean it!'	[23] Teschek, bedien' dich!

(almost tenderly)

'Take some — I mean it!'	Teschek, bedien' dich!'

(full of majesty)

'Take some — I mean it!'	Teschek, bedien, dich!'

He reaches for his fur coat, hat and cane.

ZDENKA
(entering)

I heard you call me, Papa.	Hast du gerufen, Papa?

WALDNER
(jubilant)

'Take some, take some — I mean it!' 'Waldner! Comrade! Take some — I mean it!	[23] Teschek, bedien' dich! Teschek, bedien' dich!'

ZDENKA

You are talking — to whom? What's the matter with you?	Mit wem sprichst du, Papa? Ist dir etwas gescheh'n?

WALDNER
(only now noticing that he is not alone)

Nothing. I am going out. My friends are waiting.	[23] Gar nichts. Ich geh' jetzt aus. Ich werd' erwartet.

(waving the bill at her)

'May I suggest?' Perhaps I'd better change it. Adieu.	Brauchst du vielleicht? Ich werd' mir wechseln lassen. Adieu!

Exit through the central door.

ZDENKA
(alone)

Papa! Where do you go?	[12] Papa! Er ist schon fort.
He has never behaved like that.	So hab' ich ihn noch nie geseh'n,
His worries were so great that he has lost his mind!	Die Sorgen haben ihn um den Verstand gebracht!
We cannot stay, we must leave town tomorrow,	Wir müssen fort aus dieser Stadt — schon morgen.
and dear Matteo I shall never, never see again.	Und den Matteo seh' ich heut vielleicht zum letzten Mal.
O Lord, please do help a desperate girl.	[12] O Gott, steh' mir armen Mädel bei!

Matteo enters quickly and stealthily. Zdenka is frightened.

75

I kept out of his way. When he went out, I was behind the door.	Er hat mich nicht geseh'n. Ich hab' mich rückwärts in die Tür gedrückt.

ZDENKA
(pointing to the door on the left)

Psst! She is there —	Pst! sie ist da!

(listening)

she's calling!	Sie ruft mich!

MATTEO

May I see her now?	Kann ich sie nicht sehn?

ZDENKA

Not now. You'd better not. Not now.	Jetzt nicht! Ich bitte dich! Jetzt nicht!

MATTEO

Where is my note?	Hast du den Brief?

ZDENKA

A note? Yes! No! She did not write. She says you'll have a note this evening. Come, come to the Coachmen's Ball. Before that, stay at home, in the hotel. Perhaps . . . I'll come upstairs . . . and bring it. Somehow you will get it there.	[13] Den Brief? Ja! Nein! Sie will jetzt nicht. Sie sagt, sie will ihn dir — heut abend — komm auf den Fiakerball — und vorher sei zu Haus, hier im Hotel — vielleicht bring' ich ihn dir ins Zimmer — oder du bekommst ihn dort!

MATTEO

Don't leave me in the lurch. I have your word!	Du, lass mich nicht im Stich! Ich hab' dein Wort!

Zdenka anxiously points to the door. Matteo leaves quickly. Arabella comes back in another dress, another coat, and a different hat. Zdenka is embarrassed and confused. The sleigh-bells are heard again.

ARABELLA

You are not ready? Why, what can you have been doing all this time? You'd better hurry up! The horses stamp their feet impatiently.	Bist du nicht fertig! Ja, was hast du denn gemacht die ganze Zeit? So zieh' dich endlich an! Die Rappen sind schon voller Ungeduld.

ZDENKA

The horses — and your Elemer!	[20] Die Rappen — und dein Elemer!

Furious, she leaves the room.

ARABELLA
She sits. [13, 15, 7]

My Elemer! Two words so simple yet so very strange . . . He mine — I his. I . . . his? But what is this? My heart beats as though sudden fear had overcome me . . . and such a longing . . . long . . . for what in all this world?	Mein Elemer! — das hat so einen sonderbaren Klang . . . Er mein — ich sein. Was ist denn das, mir ist ja, wie wenn eine Angst mich überfiele — und eine Sehnsucht . . . ja, nach was denn auf der Welt.

She stands up.

Long for Matteo? Just because he says he cannot live if I don't love him and implores me with eyes as big as a child's?	[12] Nach dem Matteo? Weil er immer sagt, er kann nicht leben ohne mich und mich so anschaut mit Augen wie ein Kind?

She reflects.

But for Matteo there's no longing in me.	Nach dem Matteo sehnt sich nichts in mir!

(hesitating, then breaking out)

I'd like to see that stranger again — once [7] more to see him!	Ich möchte meinen fremden Mann einmal noch sehen!
I'd like to know what it is like to hear him . . . hear him speaking.	Ich möchte einmal seine Stimme hören! Seine Stimme.
Then — then he'd just be like anyone to me.	Dann, dann wär' er wie die anderen für mich —
Zdenka says often that we must be patient till we're somebody's choice.	Wie sagt die Zdenka: dass wir warten müssen, bis uns einer wählt,
If not, no-one can save us.	und sonst sind wir verloren.
I, married to Count Elemer?	[17] Verheirat't mit dem Elemer?

She shivers involuntarily.

Why does that stir me so, as though I walked across a grave?	Was rührt mich denn so an, als trät' ich einem übers Grab?
Is that the stranger's fault, to whom I never spoke a single word?	Ist das der fremde Mann, mit dem ich nie ein Wort geredet hab',
Does he bewitch me from the dark?	zieht der im Dunkel so an mir?
My God, I'm almost sure that he must be a [7,17] married man.	Herr Gott, er ist ja sicher ein verheirateter Mann,
And I may . . . and I shall have seen the last of him!	und ich soll, und ich werd' ihn nicht mehr wiedersehn!
Today . . . today is Carnival, and tonight it is *my* party, my ball,	Und heut und heut ist Faschingsdienstag, und heut abend ist mein Ball
and I shall be its reigning Queen! And then . . .	— von dem bin ich die Königin und dann . . .

Zdenka comes back, in a short fur coat, hat in hand.

ZDENKA

Now I am ready.	So, ich bin fertig.

ARABELLA

Come.	Komm!

Zdenka opens the door and Arabella walks out. Zdenka puts her hat on and follows her. [5, 9, 10, 19] *The sleigh-bells are still heard.*

Curtain.

Norma Burrows as Zdenka at ENO, 1980 (photo: Clive Barda)

Act Two

A public ballroom, sumptuous in the style of the 1860s, with a great staircase in the centre. Arabella, with Adelaide behind her, escorted by several gentlemen, is seen slowly walking down the stairs. Waldner and Mandryka stand at the foot of the staircase. [24, 14, 5]

MANDRYKA

This is an angel whom the heavens sent to us!

Das ist ein Engel, der vom Himmel niedersteigt!

WALDNER

We're waiting! Never less than twenty minutes too late!

[23] Na, endlich! Immer eine halbe Stunde zu spät!

MANDRYKA

Oh, Waldner, Waldner!

O Waldner, Waldner!

WALDNER

If you squeeze my hand like this, How will I hold my cards when my friends [1] insist on playing? [2] Now come! I'll introduce you. Why are [18] you drawing back?

Wenn du meine Hand so druckst, werd' ich drei Tage lang keine Karten halten können, Jetzt komm! Ich stell' dich vor! Was gehst du denn zurück!

Adelaide and Arabella have arrived at the foot of the stairs. The gentlemen escorting them have stayed behind.

ADELAIDE
(softly, to Arabella)

He stands there. Is he not an elegant man? Or did I say too much?

Dort steht er. Findest du ihn elegant? Hab' ich zuviel gesagt?

ARABELLA
(seeming not to look at him) [7, 20]

Mama . . . this is a moment . . . of decision!

Mama — das ist jetzt wirklich die Entscheidung!

ADELAIDE

You are so pale. Are you not well, my child? You want to sit down? Want to leave?

Du bist sehr blass! Ist dir nicht wohl, mein Kind? Willst du dich setzen? Willst du fort?

ARABELLA

No, no, Mama.
Give me a moment's rest — leave me alone.

Nein, lass Mama.
Nur einen Augenblick lass mich allein.

Adelaide walks towards Mandryka and Waldner.

WALDNER

What is it?

Was ist denn?

ADELAIDE

Let her have a moment's rest.

Lass ihr einen Augenblick!

WALDNER

But what for?

Zu was denn?

ADELAIDE

It is only some anxiety. You know — she is like that.

Eine plötzliche Beklommenheit. Du kennst ihre Natur.

WALDNER

This is no time for her caprices!   Jetzt ist nicht Zeit für solche Faxen!
Let me introduce Herr von Mandryka.   Hier stell' ich dir vor Herrn von Mandryka.

Adelaide gives Mandryka her hand, which he kisses.

ARABELLA
(joining them)

Mama, I'm ready.   [24] Mama, da bin ich.

WALDNER
(introducing Arabella)

. . . and my daughter Arabella.   Meine Tochter Arabella.

Mandryka makes a deep bow. Adelaide draws Waldner aside. They disappear to the right.
Mandryka looks at Arabella, unable to say a word. [5, 17]

ARABELLA

You do not look like someone who would   Sie seh'n nicht aus wie jemand, den das
     care about all of this.   alles da interessiert.
(fanning herself)
I wonder what brought you here . . .   Was führt Sie denn hierher?

MANDRYKA

To Vienna?   Nach Wien?

ARABELLA

No, here, here to this ball.   Hierher auf diesen Ball!

MANDRYKA

You're asking me why I have come here,   Sie fragen mich, was mich hierherführt,
     Countess Arabella?   Gräfin Arabella?

DOMINIK
(enters and walks up to Arabella)

May I suggest we dance a waltz together?   Darf ich vielleicht um einen Walzer bitten?

ARABELLA

Later. Right now, you see, I am not free.   Später, jetzt sprech' ich hier mit diesem
     Herrn.
Dominik leaves.

MANDRYKA

It seems your father did not speak to you?   So hat Ihr Vater Ihnen nichts gesagt?

ARABELLA
(sitting down and inviting Mandryka to sit beside her)

And what was he supposed to tell me?   Was hätte er mir sagen sollen?

ELEMER
(enters and walks up to Arabella)

May I suggest we dance this waltz together?   Darf ich vielleicht um diesen Walzer
     bitten?

ARABELLA

Later. Now I stay here.   Später. Jetzt bleib' ich hier!
Elemer bows and leaves. Arabella turns to Mandryka.
I'm curious what my father was to tell me.   Was hätte mir mein Vater sagen sollen?

MANDRYKA

You've never heard of me?   Sie wissen nichts von mir?
Arabella shakes her head.
I had a lovely wife, as kind as angels are.   Ich habe eine Frau gehabt, sehr schön,
     sehr engelsgut.

but I was not allowed to stay beside her,
and after two years, God in Heaven called
her home.
I was too young, and not yet good enough
for such an angel.

Sie ist zwei Jahre nur bei mir geblieben.
Dann hat der Herrgott sie zu sich gerufen
schnell.
Zu jung war ich und noch nicht gut genug
für solchen Engel.

He lowers his head.

ARABELLA
(after a short pause)

And that is what my father was supposed [17,13]
to tell me?

Ist es das, was mein Vater mir erzählen
sollte?

MANDRYKA
(gravely)

Forgive me, please, I'm really half a peasant. [23]
With me all things are slow, but they are
strong.

Verzeihen Sie, ich bin ein halber Bauer,
bei mir geht alles langsam, aber stark.

(with sudden determination)

And I bow to your beauty, for even on [5, 7]
pictures,
your lovely face can set a heart to kindle!

Sie sind schön, Arabella — Ihr schönes
Gesicht —
auch auf dem Bild verbrennt es schon die
Seele!

ARABELLA
(frowning)

I wonder how it is that down in your [13]
Slavonia
my picture can be found?

Wie kommt man eigentlich da drunten in
Slawonien
zu einem Bild von mir?

MANDRYKA
He looks at her.

You wonder how it is . . . but no-one cares.
You're beautiful — there is a power in [21]
your lovely features
that will impress them on a soul as on
molten wax.
And for a man who is simple, who lives
with his woods and his meadows,
such a power is very great, and he is like a
dreamer,
like one obsessed with his passion. And
thus, deep in his heart he's determined,
his decision is made, and once he's made
up his mind, nothing can change it!

Wie man zu einem Bild — das ist ja gleich!
So schön sind Sie — eine Gewalt ist in
Ihren Zügen,
sich einzudrücken in die Seele wie weiches
Wachs!
Über den einfachen Menschen, den Felder
und Wälder umgeben,
ist eine solche Gewalt sehr gross, und er
wird wie ein Träumer,
wie ein Besessener wird er, und er fasst den
Entschluss mit der Seele,
einen ganzen Entschluss, und wie er
entschlossen ist, so muss er handeln!

Arabella, frightened by his outburst, gets up.

Countess, it seems I've forgotten the world
and what its ways are.

Gräfin, ich habe vergessen, wie anderswo
die Welt ist.

(getting up)

Here I'm not in my woods, on my [18]
meadows. I hope you'll forgive
all the things that I have told you, by
which I have kept you from dancing.

Hier sind nicht meine Wälder und Felder,
Sie müssen verzeihen
meine unschicklichen Reden, womit ich
Sie hind're am Tanzen.

LAMORAL
(walking up to Arabella)

May I disturb you? Could we dance this
waltz together? [13]

Darf ich jetzt stören und um einen Walzer
bitten?

ARABELLA

No. Later, Lamoral. I'd like to continue
talking to this stranger,
if he — perhaps — would kindly take a seat
again?

Nein. Später, Lamoral, ich möcht' mit
dem Herrn da noch ein biss'l reden,
wenn er — vielleicht — sich wieder
niedersetzen wird.

Lamoral bows and leaves. Arabella sits down again and motions to Mandryka to do the same. [17, 7, 21]

You want to marry me, says my father. [13] Sie wollen mich heiraten, sagt mein Vater,
But do you have an inkling who we are? Ja, haben Sie denn eine Ahnung, wer wir
 sind?

We are not very much in the eyes of the [3] Wir sind nicht grad' sehr viel, nach dem
 world, Mass dieser Welt —
we simply run along — some even think wir laufen halt so mit als etwas zweifel-
 we're rather dubious people! hafte Existenzen.

MANDRYKA

Where you come from, Arabella, Ihren Stammbaum, Arabella,
that is engraved on your face for the world den tragen Sie in Ihrem Gesicht
 to read it. geschrieben!
And if you are contented to be master over Und wenn ihnen genug ist, über einen zu
 one gebieten,
who himself is master over many, der selbst wieder gebietet über viele,
then you must come with me, and reign as so kommen Sie mit mir und seien die
 the mistress. Herrin.
There will be peacocks grazing on the Sie werden Pfauen weiden auf seid'nem
 silken ground, Boden,
and no-one ever dares believe that und das wird nicht geschehen, dass sich
 someone could be above you — jemand dünkt über Ihnen,
none but the King and the Emperor, and es sei denn der König und Kaiser und seine
 she who shares his throne! — No-one else Kaiserin! — Aber sonst niemand!
 could be!

ARABELLA
(to herself)

The one who's right — that's what I often Der Richtige — so hab' ich still zu mir
 told myself — gesagt,
the one who's right, if there is one for me, [7] der Richtige, wenn's einen gibt für mich,
one day he'll stand before me — that is der wird auf einmal da sein, so hab' ich
 what I said — gesagt,
his eyes upon me, mine on him. und wird mich anschau'n und ich ihn,
And no more subterfuges will remain, and und keine Winkelzüge werden sein und
 no more asking. keine Fragen,
No! All is light and open, like a glittering nein, alles hell und offen, wie ein lichter
 stream under a radiant sun! Fluss, auf den die Sonne blitzt!

MANDRYKA

And thus the quiet Danube glitters, flowing So fliesst die helle stille Donau mir beim
 by my house; Haus vorbei,
and it brought you to me, most beautiful [26] und hat mir dich gebracht! Du
 of all! Allerschönste! —
(mysteriously)
This very evening, at sleeping time, Und heute abend noch, zur Schlafenszeit,
if you were living in a village, one I call my wärst du ein Mädchen aus den Dörfern,
 own, einem meinigen,
you'd go and kneel beside the well that's [25] du müsstest mir zum Brunnen gehen
 behind your father's house, hinter deines Vaters Haus
and draw a drink of water — just one und klares Wasser schöpfen einen Becher
 goblet-full — voll
for me, who's standing by the threshold. und mir ihn reichen vor der Schwelle, dass
 Thus I'd be betrothed to you, ich dein Verlobter bin vor Gott
and God would be our witness, lovely und vor den Menschen, meine
 Arabella! Allerschönste!

ARABELLA

Such as you are, no-one whom I have [25] So wie Sie sind, so hab' ich keinen
 known has ever been. Menschen je geseh'n!
Around you there is such an aura of your Sie bringen Ihre eigne Lebensluft mit sich,
 own,
and anything that's strange to it has und was nicht Ihnen zugehört, das ist
 simply never been! nicht da für Sie.

MANDRYKA

To make my life worth living, something very beautiful	[21] Darum kann ich erst leben, wenn ich etwas Herrliches
must be my shining goal. And thus I now exalt you	erhöhe über mich, und so in dieser Stunde
to reign over me, and I elect you for my wife.	erhöhe ich dich, und wähle dich zu meiner Frau,
And where I am master, there you shall command,	und wo ich Herr bin, wirst du Herrin sein
and you'll be mistress of those over whom I reign!	und wirst gebieten, wo ich der Gebieter bin!

ARABELLA

My lord and master you shall be, obedient I to you.	[26] Und du wirst mein Gebieter sein, und ich dir untertan.
Your house will be my house, and in your grave I shall be resting next to you.	Dein Haus wird mein Haus sein, in deinem Grab will ich mit dir begraben sein —
I give myself to you for all the times to come.	so gebe ich mich dir auf Zeit und Ewigkeit.

(changing her tone, but serious)

But now you must be going home. I'm asking you to leave.	[13] Jetzt aber fahren Sie nach Haus. Ich bitte Sie darum.

MANDRYKA

And you?	Und Sie?

ARABELLA

I'm staying on.	Ich bleibe noch.

Mandryka bows.

I'd like to dance a while,	Ich möchte tanzen noch und Abschied nehmen
before I'm parting from the girl I was.	von meiner Mädchenzeit, nur eine Stunde lang.
Only an hour or two; can you agree to that?	Gewähren Sie mir dies?

MANDRYKA

If you are staying, then I must stay.	Wenn Sie hierbleiben.
My place is nowhere else.	[24] so ist mein Platz nicht anderswo als hier.

Arabella frowns. [13]

But you don't have to say a single word to me all evening!	Sie aber brauchen nicht ein einz'ges Wort an mich zu richten!

A swarm of coachmen and other guests appear, among them Fiakermilli, some other girls and the three Counts. [5]

ARABELLA
(looking at Mandryka)

May I?	Darf ich?

MANDRYKA

I think so, yes. You may if you are sure you want it.	Sie dürfen! Ja! Sie dürfen alles, was Sie wollen!

He steps to one side and leaves the way free for those approaching. Fiakermilli, a pretty girl in a very loud evening dress, with a bunch of flowers in her hand, walks up to Arabella, who is now standing centre stage.

DOMINIK
(standing next to Fiakermilli)

The ball is crying for its reigning queen!	Der Ball begehrt nach seiner Königin.
And Milli here will speak for the coachmen:	Der Milli ist der Herold der Fiaker,
we want to pay our respects through Milli's pretty mouth!	wir haben unsre Huldigung ihr in den Mund gelegt!

(handing her flowers to Arabella with a curtsey; frivolous, almost insolent)

Our Vienna men have studied	Die Wiener Herrn verstehn sich
all the heavenly bodies.	auf die Astronomie:
They all could be astronomers;	die könnten von der Sternwart sein
they know the how and the why.	und wissen gar nicht wie!
When there appears a brand new star,	Sie finden einen neuen Stern
they soon find out (that's how they are!)	gar schnell heraus, die Wiener Herr'n,
and name that star the Reigning Queen	den machen sie zur Königin
up in the Vienna sky!	an ihrem Firmament!
So let us tell you, one and all:	Zu der dann schallt es im Verein:
we want you to be Queen of this ball!	[5] Du sollst unseres Festes Königin sein!

CHORUS

So let us tell you, one and all,	Zu der dann schallt es im Verein:
that we have chosen you as Queen of this ball!	Du sollst unseres Festes Königin sein.

The end of Fiakermilli's song turns into exuberant yodelling, which in turn leads to the waltz. Arabella, to the strains of the waltz, takes flowers out of Fiakermilli's bunch and distributes them among the coachmen and other guests. Finally, she takes Dominik's arm and disappears into the background, followed by the crowd. Mandryka looks after her and then turns around. Adelaide returns and Matteo enters at the same moment. Zdenka steals in timidly behind Matteo. She is still dressed as a boy, in a black evening suit.

ADELAIDE
(going up to Mandryka)

You are alone? Where is Arabella?	[3] Sie sind allein? Wo ist Arabella?

MANDRYKA

Where duty bids her be — as Queen of all the coachmen!	Wo ihre Pflicht sie ruft, als Königin des Balles.

MATTEO
(into the air)

Not one thought for me — enwrapped in her beauty!	Wie sie mich vergisst — im Rausch ihrer Schönheit!

ZDENKA

She thinks of you, I know it, Matteo,	Sie denkt an dich, ich weiss es, Matteo!
but her glances don't say what she feels.	Ihre Blicke nur nimmt sie in acht.

ADELAIDE
(to Mandryka)

How your eyes are shining! What can be the reason?	Ihre Augen leuchten. Wie darf ich das deuten?

MANDRYKA
(addressing Adelaide)

Oh, Countess, dear Countess, so young still, so charming,	O Gräfin, Sie selber so jung noch, so reizend —
and you are her mother! What words could ever,	und Sie ihre Mutter! Mit was für Worten, —
what poor human words could convey enough feeling to thank you?	womit denn auf Erden vermöchte ich Ihnen zu danken!

He kisses Adelaide's hand.

MATTEO
(stepping forward)

For all she has flowers! For all she is smiling!	Die Blumen für alle! Für alle ihr Lächeln!
To all she surrenders! What's left for me?	Sie selber für alle! Was bleibt für mich?

ZDENKA
(tenderly, but tactfully to Matteo)

For you? All! All that matters. She must
  have your sadness,
deep as a draw-well.
She will trust her soul to the depths of
  sadness.
They all are shallow!

Für dich bleibt alles; sie braucht deine
  Trauer,
tief wie ein Brunnen,
ihre ganze Seele hineinzuwerfen —

seicht sind die andern!

ADELAIDE
(to Mandryka)

Oh, if I could tell you what my feelings are!
My son! My friend!
Too much, too much for my heart! I want
  to share it.
To her! To him! He has to embrace you!

O, könnten Sie ahnen, was in mir vorgeht!
Mein Sohn! Mein Freund!
Zuviel, zuviel für mein Herz. Ich muss es
  teilen.
Zu ihr, zu ihm! Er muss Sie umarmen!

Mandryka wants to follow her.

No, you'd better stay. I'll look for him.

Nein, bleiben Sie hier! Ich finde ihn!

She leaves hastily.

MATTEO
(to himself)

This remains — parting for ever!
I must forget her, if I still can.

Eines bleibt: fort nach Galizien
und sie vergessen — wenn ich noch kann!

ZDENKA
(still hiding, trying not to be seen)

She will come with Papa. I must not be
  seen.
Do not leave me, Matteo!

Der Papa! Die Mama! Dass keines mich
  sieht!
Wohin gehst du, Matteo?

Matteo walks towards the back and stares sadly into the ballroom. Adelaide and Waldner appear and go up to Mandryka. Zdenka leaves.

ADELAIDE

O Theodor! I found him, Theodor!

O Theodor! Hier ist er, Theodor!

WALDNER
(jovially)

Don't stand there like that. You look like [18]
  my old friend Mandryka.
Come, nephew, embrace your friend! [23]

Wie stehst ⌣ ⌣ vor mir, Neveu meines alten
  Mandryka?
Na, Teschek! Umarm mich schon!

He embraces Mandryka.

MANDRYKA

A table over here — I'm ordering supper.

Hierher einen Tisch. Wir werden soupieren.

A waiter with a menu appears from nowhere. Mandryka addresses Adelaide.

What are we drinking? What kind of
  champagne?

Welchen Champagner? Befehlen Sie selbst!

The waiter presents the wine list to Adelaide.

ADELAIDE

Moët-Chandon, half dry, half sweet —
  that's what we drank at my engagement.

Moët-Chandon, halb herb, halb süss —
  der war es bei meiner Verlobung!

WALDNER
(to Mandryka)

I'll join you in just a few moments.

Ich stehe sofort zur Verfügung!

He is about to leave but Adelaide holds him back.

Leave me . . . I must . . . I'm in luck!

Lass mich, ich bin im Gewinn!

He rushes off.

MANDRYKA

Thirty bottles of this one!	[23] Dreissig Flaschen von diesem!

(pointing at the wine list)

Six over here!	Sechs für den Tisch.
And another thirty!	Und noch einmal dreissig!
For everybody!	herumservieren!
Welko, go to it! Ice-buckets in every corner,	Welko, du ordnest! Eiskübel in jede Ecke!
until everyone here no longer remembers	Bis sie alle im Saal da nimmermehr wissen,
if he's a noble disguised as a Vienna coachman,	ob sie sind Grafen, verhext in Fiaker-kutscher,
or else a Vienna coachman feeling grand like a noble!	oder Fiakerkutscher, ungekrempelt in Grafen!
They ought to be happy when I am happy!	Sie sollen sich freuen, wenn ich mich freue!

(to Adelaide)

Your further orders?	Befehlen weiter!

ADELAIDE

While further lobsters, pheasants, ice-cream and other delicacies are being carried in.

Don't we have flowers?	Haben wir Blumen?

MANDRYKA
(calling)

Listen, Djura!	Aufpassen, Djura!
Go, get a carriage! And then get another! [22]	Nimmst einen Fiaker und noch einen zweiten;
Knock at the door of gardeners and florists,	aufsperren lasst die Gärtnergeschäfte,
wake up all those good-looking flower-vendors —	aufwecken die hübschen Verkäuferinnen,
tell them to clean out all their cellars!	ausräumen sollen sie ihre Keller!
One of your coaches fill with roses,	Füllst einen Wagen an mit Rosen,
and fill the other with red and white camellias!	einen mit roten und weissen Kamelien!
Arabella shall dance on flowers,	Walzer soll sie auf Blumen tanzen,
fondly greeting the girl she has been.	Abschied nehmen von Mädchenzeiten!
Later, I will spread my arms out,	Später breit' ich meine Hände,
and no longer she'll dance waltzes;	sie wird nicht mehr Walzer tanzen,
on my hands she'll do her dancing! [7]	aber tanzen auf meinen Händen!

Adelaide takes Mandryka's arm and they walk towards the back. A table is brought in and prepared for a cold supper.

ARABELLA
(coming back, escorted by Dominik)

Now I must say adieu, my dear friend Dominik.	[5] Und jetzt sag' ich adieu, mein lieber Dominik.

DOMINIK

Adieu? You are not going home?	Adieu? Sie fahren schon nach Haus?

ARABELLA

Yes. This dance was the very last; we'll dance no more.	Das war jetzt unser letzter Tanz für alle Zeit.
Could be that some day we'll meet again, you and I —	Kann sein, dass wir uns später einmal wiedersehn,
then I'll be an acquaintance from the olden times.	dann sind wir halt Bekannte aus der Jugendzeit!

DOMINIK
(grasping her arm)

Arabella!	Arabella!

ARABELLA
(peacefully)

No, Dominik.

Nein, Dominik!

(shaking him off)

Among the men I knew, you were the very first
(not counting silly boys) who ever told me
That he was fond of me. I admit that I was glad.
But I could never be the one who's right [7] for you,
and you were not the one who's right for me.
Don't say it, Dominik. You see, there comes Count Elemer. Adieu!

Sie sind der erste Mann gewesen, Dominik!
— von Buben red' ich nicht — der mir gesagt hat,
dass er mich gern hat, und es hat mich recht gefreut.
Aber die Richtige für Sie, die war ich nicht,
und Sie halt nicht der Richtige für mich.
Nicht reden, Dominik. Da kommt schon auch der Elemer. Adieu!

Dominik walks away slowly.

ELEMER
(entering tempestuously) [19]

I've never seen you as lovely as tonight!
You are not quite the same.

So schön wie heut hab' ich dich nie gesehn!
Mit dir ist was passiert!

ARABELLA

Yes, Elemer, I am not quite the same.
And that is why I am holding out my hand
and say 'adieu' and 'I am grateful', Elemer.
There have been many lovely moments, I remember . . .

Ja, Elemer, mit mir ist was passiert!
Und darum geb' ich Ihnen jetzt die Hand
und sag' adieu, ich danke Ihnen, Elemer —
es waren viele schöne Augenblicke drunter —

ELEMER

There have been? Bella! There will be more!

Es waren, Bella, es werden sein!

ARABELLA

Please do not hold my hand. Just for one moment touch my fingers lightly;
remember that we are the best of friends even though we never meet again.

Nicht halten meine Hand, grad schnell den Druck von meinen Fingern spüren
und wissen, dass wir gute Freunde sind, wenn wir uns auch nicht wiedersehn!

ELEMER
(violently)

I take it you're in love with that intruder!
With that Croatian, or what he may be!

Sie haben sich verliebt in diesen Fremden!
diesen Wallachen, oder was er ist!

ARABELLA
(very quietly)

This final moment, I beg you, do not spoil for me.
You see, there comes Count Lamoral,

who's waiting to dance our final waltz.

Nicht mir verdeben diesen letzten Augenblick,
da kommt auch schon der Lamoral und wartet
auf seinen letzten Tanz!

Lamoral appears on the stairs.

ELEMER
(close by her)

I want you for my wife!
Who in this world dares ever cross my path!?

Werden Sie meine Frau!
Wer in der Welt ist, der mich hindern darf!?

ARABELLA

No, no. There is another happiness for me.

Nein. Nein. Für mich war halt ein andres Glück bestimmt.

She lets Elemer stand there and goes up to Lamoral. Elemer leaves.

LAMORAL

O Arabella! What is more beautiful than you when you are gay?

O Arabella, gibt es was Schöneres als Sie auf einem Ball!

ARABELLA

How sweet it is to play at being lovers; sweet all this make-believe!
And yet I know there's something else — much higher, more beautiful —
one day, you too may grasp it, perhaps . . .

Ja, süss ist die Verliebtheit, süss dieses Auf und Ab,
aber es gibt was Schöneres und Höh'res tausendmal!
Und einmal wirst du auch verstehn, vielleicht —

LAMORAL

Don't speak of other things to me that are far off!

Nicht reden jetzt von anderem, das weit weg ist —

ARABELLA

For you they are far off, that is quite true.

Für dich ist's noch weit weg, da hast du recht.

LAMORAL

You frighten me. You are so different, Arabella.
Someone steals you from me!

Ich änstig' mich. Sie sind so anders, Arabella.
Es nimmt Sie mir wer weg!

ARABELLA

Stealing me? Not from you! Now, be good. Come here — I will kiss you. But this kiss is the first and last.

Wegnehmen? Geh, du Bub! Aber da hast du deinen ersten und zugleich deinen letzten Kuss.

She bends her head towards him and kisses his forehead, quickly and softly. [7]

LAMORAL
(radiant)

Whose lips were these that have graced me with a kiss?

Von wem hab' ich diesen wunderbaren Kuss?

ARABELLA
(immediately disengaging herself and walking away from Lamoral)

A girl has kissed you who is so happy today . . .
so happy that she must be by herself, all alone with herself,
the world forgetting . . . to lie and dream, with eyes unclosed,
her happiness won't let her sleep!

Von einem Mädel, das heut glücklich ist,

so glücklich, dass sie ganz allein sein muss,

ganz mit sich selbst allein in ihrem Zimmer
und lang noch liegen ohne Schlaf vor lauter Glück!

(with a different voice)

Now, if you like, you may dance this last waltz with me.
But then I'll go away; you've seen the last of me!

Jetzt aber tanzen wir noch diesen Walzer aus,
dann fahr ich fort von euch auf Nimmerwiedersehn!

She leaves together with Lamoral [5, 14]. Matteo comes back. Zdenka, still anxiously trying not to be seen, stares at Matteo. [10, 12]

MATTEO

I'm such a coward! Why remain? No! No more suffering!

Ein Feigling bin ich. Fort mit mir! Fort und eine Ende!

ZDENKA

Oh, Lord, how he glowers! So grimly determined!

O Gott! Seine Miene! Wie furchtbar entschlossen!

She beckons to Matteo, who walks over to her. Mandryka returns and goes to the table that has been prepared for supper. [18] *He gives Welko a message. Zdenka speaks full of anxiety.*

Are you like that again? One of your tantrums?

Bist du schon wieder so? Hat's dich schon wieder?

MATTEO [13]

Passion consumes me!

Rasend verzehrt's mich!

ZDENKA

She thinks of you! That's all she thinks of!

Sie denkt an dich! Nichts andres denkt sie!

Matteo laughs bitterly.

Look, here, this is a letter that she wrote you.
Here, take it!

Sie hat mir einen Brief für dich gegeben!

Hier ist er.

She takes a letter out of the inside pocket of her suit.

MATTEO
(*shrinking back*)

No! Take it back!
This is her farewell for ever,
I feel it!
No! Take it back. I feel this is goodbye for me!

Ich nehm' ihn nicht!
Der bringt das Ende für immer!
Ich fühl' es!
[15] Trag ihn zurück! Ich fühl', dass es mein Abschied ist!

Zdenka follows him with the letter. Mandryka's attention is suddenly caught by what is going on. Jankel enters, followed by men carrying flowers.

ZDENKA

Come, take the letter. Things will be different.
Just touch it once.

Du musst ihn nehmen, alles wird anders!

So fühl ihn doch!

MATTEO
(*taking the letter*)

A door-key?

Ein Schlüssel?

ZDENKA

Come on! Take it, please!

Nimm ihn! Nimm ihn nur!

MATTEO
(*feverishly opening the letter*)

No note? Just a door-key?
Maybe you are joking? Zdenko, I ask you?

Kein Brief, nur ein Schlüssel?
[28] Was sind das für Spässe? Zdenko, ich frage!

ZDENKA
(*pale, almost fainting*)

It is her own key!

[27] Das ist ihr Schlüssel!

MATTEO

Her own key?

[27] Ihr Schlüssel?

ZDENKA

The key to ... her room! Don't show it!

Vom Zimmer. Gib acht. Versteck ihn.

MATTEO

It is her door-key? I must be demented!

Are we at a ball? Are you her brother?

And she is your sister? She's dancing back there?
And this is her key?

[6] Das ist der Schlüssel? — Ich bin nicht bei Sinnen!
Sind wir auf dem Ball? Bist du der Zdenko?
[5] Ist sie deine Schwester? Sie tanzt dort unten?
[27] Das ist der Schlüssel?

You can believe me: Zu ihrem Zimmer!
(spoken)
It is the key to Arabella's room.   Der Schlüssel zu Arabellas Zimmer!

MANDRYKA
(wincing; also spoken)

My ears deceive me!   Ich hab' mich verhört!

Jankel approaches Mandryka, who waves him away and moves closer to Zdenka and Matteo.

ZDENKA
(spoken)

You must go home. She'll be there in a   Du sollst nach Haus — sie kommt in einer
quarter of an hour.   Viertelstunde.
The key opens the room next to hers!   Der Schlüssel sperrt das Zimmer neben
                                 ihrem.
(now blushing, now pale; sung)
she'll be coming to you in silence, [5, 12, 28]Lautlos kommt sie zu dir — Matteo, sie
                              will nicht,
she does not want you to be so sad. She'll   dass du unglücklich bist! — Sie will alles
do anything,   [6, 11, 15]   tun, alles,
only to give you happiness, this very   damit du glücklich wirst noch diese Nacht!
night.

MATTEO

Swear you are not lying!   [28]   Schwör mir, dass wahr ist,
This key is for Arabella's bedroom?   Der Schlüssel zu Arabellas Zimmer!

ZDENKA

Yes, that is true! And this is true: Du hast ihn ja, so wahr er sperrt,
that she who gave this key to you,   [27]   so wahr will die, die ihn dir gibt,
will give you everything to make you   [12]   heut alles tun, damit du glücklich wirst!
happy.
Now I must go. They must not see me   Ich muss jetzt fort! Mich darf man hier
here.   nicht sehn!

She runs off.

MATTEO
(to himself)

Mysterious is the heart of woman, and   Geheimnis eines Mädchenherzens,
unfathomable!   unergründliches!

He leaves.

MANDRYKA
(suddenly rousing himself from his immobility)

Hey, you! Anybody! Anyone will do!   [6]   Halt! Du irgendeiner oder wer du bist!
Welko! Djura! Go and stop that man   Welko, Djura! Halten dort den Menschen!
there!
Bring him here to me — the one with the   Her mit ihm vor mich! Den dort mit dem
door-key.   Schlüssel!

Dominik enters with Adelaide. Welko and Djura are uncertain whom their master has in mind.

WELKO

Which one, Gospodar?   Welchen, Gospodar?

DJURA

Which one do you mean?   Und was für einen?

WELKO
(pointing at Dominik)

This one?   Diesen?
Dominik and Adelaide sit down on a sofa.

MANDRYKA
(to himself)

Perhaps there's more than one called Arabella,	[5] Und wenn hier viele Arabella heissen —
or my god-forsaken hunter's ears have played me false — I'm such a stupid peasant!	meine gottverdammten Jägerohren foppen meinen dummen harten Schädel,
What a perfect fool I'd make before a stranger!	— dass ich als ein Narr da steh' vor einem Fremden?
Would she send her key to someone in this ballroom,	[27] Wird sie denn den Schlüssel schicken von dem Zimmer,
while she herself is dancing gaily?	während sie selber tanzt im Ballsaal?

(looking at his watch)

Still those final moments are not over that I granted her to spend in dancing.	Noch ist nicht einmal vorbei die Stunde, die ich grad' ihr freigegeben habe —
Yet I am already fooled and cheated!	Also bin ich schon ein Narr und Esel?

(addressing his three servants)

Just forget it! Set the table for our supper.	Alles lassen! Weitermachen dort am Esstisch!

(pacing up and down)

Music is a dream — no key is in it!	[18] Schön ist die Musik, und nichts von Schlüssel,
Violins — no cursed key is in them!	Geigen drin, und nicht verdammte Schlüssel,
It won't be very long now; she will stand here,	und in ein paar Minuten wird sie dastehn,
and a thousand flowers will be strewn here,	da vor mir, und Blumen werd' ich hinstreu'n,
and in my stead they will kiss her ankles.	dass statt meiner sie den Fuss ihr küssen.
Let her have her dance! This is the moment	May! Wie tanzt sie jetzt und nimmt den Abschied
when she is parting from the girl she was.	in dieser Stunde von der Mädchenzeit!

DOMINIK
(to Adelaide)

How enchanting you are! The mother outshining the daughter...	O bezaubernde Frau! Viel schöner als jemals die Tochter!
You could always cure my heart when I am melancholy.	Wie Sie die Melancholie mir zu heilen verstünden —

He kisses her shoulder.

ADELAIDE
(shrinking back and drawing her cape around her shoulders)

Dominik! Don't! Maybe later... I shall always be lonely without my child.	Dominik! Nicht! Aber später, ich werd' immer allein sein ohne mein Kind —

They go on talking softly. Several couples appear from the ballroom.

MANDRYKA
(with a grim glance)

But why all these people? Only she is missing.	Warum kommen viele und nicht sie darunter?
And why is it that those cursed keys go on rattling?	Warum scheppern gottverdammte Schlüssel dazwischen?

Fiakermilli enters on Elemer's arm. She walks up to Mandryka, followed by some other couples.

FIAKERMILLI

Now please! Once more I must approach you and ask you: don't deprive the ball of her — its reigning queen!	Mein Herr, schon wieder muss ich kommen und bitten: Geben Sie dem Ball die Königin zurück!

(furious, to himself)

What does she say, that female? I must not deprive them of her? But I did not lock her up!	Was sagt das Frauenzimmer? Ich soll sie zurück ihr geben? Ich hab' sie nicht eingesperrt.
I do not have the key — it's in that envelope!	Ich hab' den Schlüssel nicht. Er ist in dem Kuvert.

He clutches an armchair so roughly that the arms break. Welko serves champagne. Mandryka takes a glass. [15, 23]

I ask you, will you be my guests, and give me the honour —	Ich bitte, dass Sie mir die Ehre geben —
all of you — both friends and those unknown!	[19] Sie alle, wie Sie sind, bekannt und unbekannt.

ELEMER

But where is Arabella? All of us miss her this joyous night. We must remind her!	[5] Doch Gräfin Arabella wollen wir nicht in dem schönen Augenblick vermissen!
We're sure that you must know where you can find her!	[22] Sie werden sicher sie zu finden wissen.

MANDRYKA
(wrenching at his tie)

Where can I find her? Door-key! Djura! Welko!	Zu finden wissen? Schlüssel! Djura! Welko!

Welko and Djura come running.

Look for the Countess everywhere you can!	Die gnädige Fräulein suchen in dem Saal!
If you have found her in this giant Vienna town,	Habt's ihr gefunden in der grossen Wienerstadt,
I'm sure that you can find her in a dance-hut such as this!	werd's ihr zu finden wissen in der Tanzhütten dahier!

Welko and Djura leave. Mandryka shouts after them:

And ask her to come here, if she will be so very kind.	— und bitte sie hierher, wenn sie die Gnade haben will!

He turns to Fiakermilli, who has moved away from Elemer.

A mouth as sweet as this one shall only drink the sweetest!	Ein solcher süsser Schnabel muss auch was Süsses trinken!

He offers her a glass of champagne. At the same time, Jankel approaches, bringing a letter on a tray.

JANKEL

Here is a note for your Excellency.	Da wäre ein Billett für Euer Gnaden.

MANDRYKA

See whether there's a key in it!	Fühl, ob ein Schlüssel drin ist.

JANKEL

A key?	Wie, ein Schlüssel?

MANDRYKA
(taking the letter hastily but hesitating before opening it)

Who, my Lord, who gave to this face such a tremendous power over me	Wer, Herr Gott, hat diesem Gesicht so viel Gewalt gegeben über mich,
that I am so afraid?	[23] dass ich mich fürchte jetzt? —

He tears the envelope open and reads.

'For now I say to you "goodnight" — I'm going home.	Für heute sag' ich Ihnen gute Nacht, ich fahr' nach Haus.
From tomorrow on, I shall be yours.'	von morgen an bin ich die Ihrige.
A small 'a' instead of a signature!	[14] Ein kleines A statt einer Unterschrift!
She did not even sign it! It's not worth her while	Nicht einmal ihren Namen. Steht auch nicht dafür
for one so simple-minded that he fell for all her wiles!	für einen Gimpel, einen auf den Leim gegangenen!

It's true: tonight she's parting from the girl
  she was —
for that she must keep all her tenderness.
Therefore she has no time to write a tender
  signature.

He forces himself to appear brash and gay, and joins the others.

Out of my sight these flowers! More
  champagne!
I'll treat you left and right, till all of you are
  too drunk to stand —
the nobles, the coachmen, the coachmen's
  sweethearts — and all of you together!
Let's go on drinking, bottle after bottle. [26]

You are all invited. [27]

The waiters bow and serve champagne to everybody.

Perhaps the lovely Milli would like me to
  sing one?

(taking Fiakermilli in his arms)

I'm in the mood for it!

Fiakermilli answers tenderly and wordlessly, with a yodel. Mandryka continues, torn between tears and fury.

Walking through the woods, don't know [22, 26]
  through which one,
found a girl there, don't know who's her
  father.
I stepped on her foot, don't know which
  one.
She began to cry, don't know the reason!

'Look at him — he thinks he knows what
  love is!'

Mandryka draws Fiakermilli to his side on the sofa.

FIAKERMILLI

Look at him, he thinks he knows what love
  is!

Adelaide gets up and moves away from Dominik.

MANDRYKA

Would be good to give him wine in barrels,

wine in barrels. Not to give him any cup.
Let him drink his wine right from the
  barrel.
Let him rough it, till one day he may love
  it!

FIAKERMILLI
(yodelling the refrain)

Let him rough it, till one day he may love
  it!

MANDRYKA

It would be good (so said the girl) if I'd
  surrender,
if I'd surrender. But my bed I'll not
  surrender!

(grimly)

Let him sleep and snore right on the wood-
  planks.
Let him rough it, till one day he may love
  it!

Fiakermilli yodels the refrain. Mandryka gets up abruptly.

Sie muss ja Abschied nehmen von der
  Mädchenzeit,
dafür braucht sie die ganze Zärtlichkeit:
sie hat jetzt keine Zeit für zärtlichere
  Unterschrift!

Wegschmeissen jetzt die Blumen!
  Schampus her!
Servieren links und rechts, bis alle liegen
  unterm Tisch,
die Grafen und Fiaker und Fiakerbräute
  und alle miteinander!
Heut geht das Ganze, aber schon das
  Ganze
auf meine Rechnung!

Soll ich der schönen Milli vielleicht jetzt
  was singen?

Ich wäre aufgelegt!

Ging durch einen Wald, weiss nicht durch
  welchen!
Fand ein Mädchen, weiss nicht, wessen
  Tochter!
Trat ihr auf den Fuss, weiss nicht auf
  welchen,
fing es an zu schrei'n, weiss nicht warum
  doch,
seht den Wicht, wie der sich denkt die
  Liebe!

Seht den Wicht, wie der sich denkt die
  Liebe!

Wohl stünd's an, ihm Kanne Wein zu
  geben,
Wein zu geben, Becher nicht zu geben,
mag der Wicht aus schwerer Kanne trinken,

mag sich plagen bis zu klügeren Tagen!

Mag sich plagen bis zu klügeren Tagen!

Wohl stünde an, mich Mädchen ihm zu
  geben,
mich zu geben, doch kein Bett zu geben.

Mag der Kerl auf blosser Erde schlafen,

mag sich plagen bis zu klügeren Tagen!

Tonight she goes to meet the man who has [18]
the key.
Tomorrow, though, she'll be my one and
own.
Milli, come here and kiss me!

He kisses her.

How much
Is a door-key to a Countess's room, here in
Vienna?

Für heut fahrt sie nach Haus zu ihrem
Schlüsselherrn,
von morgen an ist sie die Meinige!
Milli, gib mir ein Bussl!

Wieviel kost't
der Schlüssel für Comtessenzimmer hier
in Wien!

ADELAIDE
(suddenly standing before him)

Herr von Mandryka, please, where is my
daughter?

Herr von Mandryka, wo ist meine Tochter?

MANDRYKA
(with Fiakermilli in his arms)

Don't know. Your daughter did not [13]
condescend
to leave a message. Care for more Moët-
Chandon?
Right here! Champagne for her most
gracious mother!

Weiss nicht! Sie hat die Gnade nicht
gehabt,
mir mitzuteilen. Wünschen noch Moët-
Chandon?
Hier ist! Servieren der Frau Gräfin Mutter!

ADELAIDE
(searching the room for Waldner)

Where is my husband? Please go and find [23]
my husband!

Wo ist mein Mann? Man suche meinen
Mann!

Dominik runs off to look for Waldner. Adelaide turns to Mandryka. [1, 2]
Once again, I implore you, where is
Arabella?

Lassen Sie sich beschwören, wo ist Arabella?

MANDRYKA
(insolently)

That's what I'm asking! Asking you, her
mother!

Das frag' ich selber die Frau Gräfin
Mutter!

*Waldner appears with Dominik. Behind him come the three gentlemen with whom he has
been playing cards.*

ADELAIDE

O Theodor!
Protect us! Yes, protect me and your
daughter!

O Theodor!
Beschütze deine Frau und deine Tochter!

WALDNER

What's going on? Mandryka, have you lost
your mind?
Please don't forget, this is my wife!

Was geht hier vor? Mandryka, wie
benimmst du dich
in Gegenwart von meiner Frau!

MANDRYKA

I act quite 'comme il faut'.
I've left behind the peasant yokel that I
was,
and now I am behaving like a noble
Vienna Count!
Sit down with us. There are girls galore!
Champagne galore!
Take some — I mean it!

Genau, wie sich's gehört!
Ich streife ab den dummen Kerl aus der
Provinz
[19] und bin, wie unter wienerischen Grafen
sich's geziemt!
Setz dich zu uns, sind Mädeln da, is
Schampus da!
Teschek, bedien dich!

WALDNER
(addressing him)

But where is my daughter?

Wo ist meine Tochter?

MANDRYKA

I'm very sorry, there I cannot help you.

Ich kann dir leider keine Auskunft geben.

They tell me, Waldner, that a Countess has her whims: once in a while she simply disappears!

Comtessen, scheint es, ziehen manchmal sich zurück in einem animierten Augenblick.

WALDNER
(*turning to Adelaide, furious*)

Where's Arabella? Will you tell me where she is? You know it!

Wo ist das Mädel? Wissen will ich, wo sie [24] ist! Du weisst es?

ADELAIDE

At home.

— zu Haus!

WALDNER

And why should she go home?

[13] Was soll das bedeuten?

ADELAIDE

Caprice . . . or a sudden attack of despair. She is so moody; you know the way she is!

Ein Einfall! Eine plötzliche Melancholie! [17] Eine Caprice! Du kennst ihr Naturell!

WALDNER

Can you swear that she is back home?

Du beschwörst, sie ist zu Hause?

ADELAIDE

Now, Theodor, remember, she is also *your* child.

Es handelt sich um deine und meine Tochter!

WALDNER

All right. Let us go home together, right this moment.
Then you will talk to her, and you'll inform us
how she is feeling, just so we won't have to worry.

Sehr gut, wir fahren auch nach Hause. Augenblicklich.
Du klopfst an ihre Tür und gibst uns Nachricht,
ob sie ganz wohl ist: nur damit wir uns beruhigen.

(*addressing Mandryka, grimly*)

And then, I'll have a word or two with you!

Dann spreche ich zwei Worte noch mit dir;

Therefore, you will now have the kindness to come along.

darum wirst du die Güte haben, uns zu begleiten.

MANDRYKA

With pleasure. I'll consider it an honour, too.

Es wird mir eine ganz besondere Ehre sein.

He bows and offers his arm to Adelaide.

WALDNER
(*to his fellow gamblers*)

We'll continue our little game at the hotel, as soon as I've taken care of this minor misunderstanding.

Wir spielen augenblicklich weiter im Hotel, sobald das kleine Missverständnis da beseitigt ist.

MANDRYKA
(*standing at the door and shouting behind him*)

And in the meantime, you make merry. I [23] invite you!

Die Herren und Damen sind einstweilen meine Gäste!

FIAKERMILLI

Eljen! We all are invited!

[19] Eljen! Wir sind Ihre Gäste!

All the guests lift their glasses. Mandryka and Adelaide leave, followed by Waldner, the gamblers, Welko and Djura.

GUESTS

Eljen! We all are invited!

[14, 18] Eljen! Wir sind Ihre Gäste!

Curtain.

94

Act Three

Prelude [5, 6, 10, 12, 15, 16]

An open room on the ground floor of the hotel. In the centre, a big staircase leads to the first floor rooms. There are a few tables with newspapers and easy chairs. It is night. Matteo, without his uniform jacket, is seen upstairs leaning over the bannisters. He seems to be looking for something. The outer doorbell is ringing. Matteo disappears. A waiter comes out of the reception room and opens the door. Arabella enters, returning from the ball. The waiter leaves. Arabella walks slowly towards the stairs. Her eyes are half-closed, her face is full of happiness. She smiles, and as though she were half dreaming, half awake, she sits down and slightly sways to the strain of the music she is singing. [7, 14]

ARABELLA

Through his fields and meadows we shall ride together,	Über seine Felder wird der Wagen fahren
riding through the high and silent forests.	und durch seine hohen, stillen Wälder —
Yes, that's where I see him: high and silent forests.	[26] ja, zu denen passt er; hohe stille Wälder;
And then, there will be his huntsmen — they will come to meet us.	[17] und dann werden seine Reiter uns entgegenkommen.
'Honour and obey her' he will tell them,	[22] 'Das ist Eure Herrin', wird er sagen,
'She's the one whom I brought here' he will tell them,	[18] 'die ich mir geholt hab', wird er sagen,
'from Imperial Vienna. But she no longer wants to go back there;	'aus der Kaiserstadt, jetzt aber will sie nimmermehr zurück —
now she wants to stay with me, and with my forests.'	bleiben will sie nur bei mir in meinen [25] Wäldern.'

Matteo appears again upstairs and leans over the railing. He sees and recognises Arabella but can hardly believe his eyes. He mutters to himself:

MATTEO

Arabella! It can't be! I cannot believe it!	Arabella! Unmöglich! Es ist ja nicht denkbar!

Arabella rouses herself from her happy dreams. She does not see Matteo, who is behind her, but she feels that she is no longer alone. Matteo has walked down the stairs and bows before Arabella.

ARABELLA
(surprised, but without any emotion)

You, here?	Sie hier?
(getting up quickly)	
So late?	So spät?
It seems you are still staying in this house.	So wohnen Sie noch immer hier im Haus?

MATTEO
(with a hidden meaning)

You here? That's what I'm asking, Arabella.	Sie hier? So muss ich fragen, Arabella!
It's very late. You're going out?	Du gehst so spät noch einmal aus?

ARABELLA

I've only just returned. I'm going to my room now. Pleasant dreams! [14, 13, 7]	Ich komme heim vom Ball und gehe auf mein Zimmer, gute Nacht!

She is about to go up the stairs, passing him by.

MATTEO
(with infinite irony)

You've only just returned! You go to your room now!	Sie kommen heim vom Ball! Sie gehn auf Ihr Zimmer?

(half to himself)

A girlish heart is full of secrets; no-one
fathoms it.

Geheimnis eines Mädchenherzens,
unergründliches!

ARABELLA

Well, pleasant dreams. I wonder why
you're so amused?

[13] Ja, gute Nacht. Was amüsiert Sie da so
sehr?

MATTEO

O Arabella!

[16] O Arabella!

He smiles amorously and suggestively.

ARABELLA

If there is something else you have to tell
me,
then speak to me by day — not now! Not
here!

Wenn Sie mir noch etwas zu sagen haben,

dann bitte ich, bei Tag, nicht jetzt, nicht
hier!

MATTEO

Something else? I . . . something else?
Oh, sweetest Arabella! Let me give you
thanks,
today, tomorrow, always, till my dying
day!

[28] Noch — etwas? Ich — noch — etwas?
O süsse Arabella, danken will ich dir

von heute bis ans Ende meines Lebens!

ARABELLA

Thank me? For what? You know that all is
over now, once and for all!

Danken — wofür? Das ist doch alles ein
für allemal vorbei.

MATTEO
(with heavy irony)

Thank you? For what? Your art escapes
my grasp!
I'm scared by so much cold-blooded skill!

Danken? Wofür? — Die Kunst ist mir zu
hoch!
Mir graut vor so viel Virtuosität.

ARABELLA

What do you mean?

Was haben Sie?

MATTEO

To make believe, and play the actress, only
for the fun of playing —
to play the actress with no audience —
that is too much! It almost looks like evil
witchcraft!

So meisterhaft Komödie spielen nur um
der Komödie willen,
Komödie spielen ohne Publikum!
Das ist zuviel! Das grenzt an böse
[10, 15] Hexenkünste!

ARABELLA

I do not understand the things that you are
telling me,
and therefore, pleasant dreams.

Von allen Ihren Reden da versteh' ich
nicht ein Wort,
und somit gute Nacht.

MATTEO
(not letting her pass)

All right. But one more glance first, all I'm
asking is one glance,
to say you are unchanging and the same!

Schon gut! Jetzt einen Blick noch, einen
einzigen, der mir sagt,
dass du im Innersten die Gleiche bist!

ARABELLA

Unchanging?

Die Gleiche?

MATTEO
(ardently)

Unchanging! Unchanging! The one you
were a little while ago still!

[28] Die Gleiche? Die Gleiche? Die Gleiche,
wie vor einer Viertelstunde!

ARABELLA
(quite innocently)

A little while ago I . . . I was somewhere   [26] Vor einer Viertelstunde war ich anderswo!
else.

MATTEO
(the expression of an enchanted memory on his face)

A little while ago you were . . . you know   Vor einer Viertelstunde! Ja! da oben!
where!

He stares at her ardently.

ARABELLA
(with a glance upstairs, not understanding)

I cannot understand you and I do not care   Ich weiss nicht, was Sie meinen, und ich
to stand around.   möchte hier nicht länger stehn!

MATTEO
(violently)

This is too much! Such cold assurance   Das ist zuviel! So kalte Herrschaft über
over every nerve —   jeden Nerv!
and after such a moment! Let me implore   Nach solchen Augenblicken — das erträgt
  kein Mann!
the one and only blood-drop that's in you   Ich appelliere an den einen Blutstropfen in
  dir,
that is unable to simulate!   der unfähig zu heucheln ist!

He grabs her arm.

ARABELLA [5, 6, 28, 15, 13]

You are out of your senses, Matteo!   Sie sind ja nicht bei Sinnen!
Do not try to hold me back — someone   Matteo! Geben Sie den Weg mir frei, oder
will hear me!   ich rufe!

MATTEO

You know how you can make me lose my   Du könntest einen Mann zum Wahnsinn
reason;   bringen,
you, like no woman in this world.   du, so wie niemand auf der Welt!
Now, look at me, and grant me only a   Bekräftige mit einem einzigen letzten
parting glance,   Blick,
to seal what happened there upstairs   was zwischen uns gewesen ist, dort oben,
between us.
And this is all I ask of you in all this world!   und nichts auf dieser Welt verlang' ich
  mehr von dir!

The waiter comes out of the reception room to open the door.

ARABELLA

I hear some people. Don't try to stop me!   Hier kommen Menschen, lassen Sie mich
  los!

MATTEO

I gave my promise that you would be free   Ich hab's geschworen, dass du frei sein
of me   wirst von mir,
after this evening. I swore it into your   [6, 10]in deine Tränen, in deine flüsternden
whispering kisses,   Küsse hab' ich's geschworen —
tears streaming down your cheeks. I will   von morgen ab! Ich halte meinen Schwur!
not break my oath!   [15, 16, 11]
But we were in darkness; I never for a   Wir waren im Dunkel, ich habe deine
moment saw your eyes.   Augen nicht gesehen.
Now give me one more glance — a glance   Gib einen Blick mir jetzt, der alles noch
that seals in parting all that has been,   zum letztenmal besiegelt,
and you are free for ever!   [7] und du bist frei für immer!

*Adelaide enters followed by Mandryka who stops abruptly. After him appear Waldner and
the three gamblers. Welko and Djura remain standing by the door.*

97

ADELAIDE

What an excited tête-à-tête, right on the stairs!

You wanted to retire, but are still downstairs?

My child, what is the reason?

[3] Welch ein erregtes tête-à-tête im Stiegenhaus!

[15] Du hast dich also zurückgezogen?

Mein Kind, was soll das heissen?

ARABELLA

Nothing's wrong Mama, nothing.

[6, 27] Aber nichts, Mama, garnichts.

MANDRYKA
(staring fixedly at Matteo)

Yes! That man is the devil of the door-key! [27] Ja. Es ist der Verfluchte mit dem Schlüssel.

ARABELLA
(taking one step towards Mandryka, without any sign of embarrassment)

I did not think I'd see you again this evening, Herr von Mandryka.

Sie hab' ich heut nicht mehr zu sehen vermutet, Herr von Mandryka!

MANDRYKA
(to Adelaide)

I ask you, Countess, for my permission to retire at once.

Ich bitte, Gräfin, um Erlaubnis, mich zurückzuziehn!

(stepping back)

Welko!

Welko!

WELKO

My Gospodar, is this the one?

Der Gospodar hat ihn erkannt?

MANDRYKA

Get packed! Tomorrow morning we are going home.

Du packst. Wir fahren mit dem ersten Zug nach Haus.

ARABELLA
(turning towards Mandryka)

Why should this be of concern to you, Mandryka?

When I came home, I met Matteo here,

a dear old friend of all of us. But all these details

I'll gladly tell you later, if you want it.

[24] Hier ist nichts, das Sie anginge, Mandryka.

Ich komm' nach Haus, begegne diesem Herrn,

das ist ein alter Freund von uns. Darüber alles

[28, 7] erzähl' ich Ihnen später, wenn Sie wollen.

MANDRYKA

I should be much obliged if you'd excuse me.

Ich bitte wirklich sehr, mich zu entschuldigen!

Mandryka is about to leave. Arabella, puzzled, shakes her head.

ADELAIDE

O Vienna! Town of evil tongues, malice and gossip!

[3, 9] O Wien! Die Stadt der Médisance und der Intrige!

(to Matteo)

You don't know *what* you've done!

Sie Unglückseliger!

WALDNER
(detaining Mandryka)

Stay here another moment, please.

It seems there are still a few misunderstandings left.

Du bleibst noch einen Augenblick!

Es scheint, dass hier noch Missverständnisse geblieben sind.

(to Arabella)

I'm asking you, my child, where have you been?

How did you get home from the ball? Did *he* escort you?

Ich frage dich, mein Kind! Wo kommst du her?

Hat der Herr Leutnant dich vom Ball nach Haus begleitet?

98

| | Did you agree to it? | Mit deiner Zustimmung? |

ARABELLA

| | Papa, please look into my eyes! | Papa, so schau mir ins Gesicht! |
How can one madman drive everybody [13] Kann ein Verrückter alle närrisch machen
   crazy in no time?   auf eins, zwei?

WALDNER

There's nothing you have to tell me?   Du hast mir nichts zu sagen?

ARABELLA

Not a single thing, [21] Aber wirklich nichts,
except the one you knew about, Papa,   als was du ohnehin schon weisst, Papa,
and knew all evening. Or perhaps you did   seit heute abend. Oder weisst du etwa
   not know?   nicht?

WALDNER

That makes me feel much better.   Da bin ich sehr erleichtert.
He kisses Arabella's forehead, then turns to Mandryka.
Use your judgement.   Also bitte!
You see, nothing has happened. Simply   Es ist nichts vorgefallen! Aber garnichts!
   nothing.
Don't worry, just forget all this to-do. And [23] Schwamm drüber über alle Aufregung,
   so goodnight.   und gute Nacht!
   (to the gamblers)
Let's go and play in there. No reason to [1, 2]Ich bitte dort hinein. Wir spielen sofort
   lose more time.   weiter.

MANDRYKA
(stepping towards Arabella, and speaking only to her)

I want to help you, if indeed good will and [6] Ich werde helfen, soviel Geld und guter
   money can be of help, [23]   Wille helfen kann,
to cover up the comedy you're playing,   vertuschen diese hässliche Komödie,
since for the role in which it seems you   da ich die Rolle nicht geeignet bin zu spielen,
   chose to cast me [5, 14]
I feel I am unsuitable, my Fräulein.   die Sie mir haben zugedacht, mein Fräulein.
   (turning away from her)
No, no! I simply can't believe it. It simply   Nein, nein, wie ist das möglich! Wie kann
   cannot be!   das möglich sein!

ADELAIDE

Oh, that threefold disgraceful encounter! [3] O dreimal unglückselige Begegnung!

WALDNER

Let's have no more arias, if you'll be so   Jetzt keine Arien, wenn ich bitten darf!
   kind.

ARABELLA [7, 6]
(only to Mandryka)

Mandryka, hear me out. As true as God on [17] Mandryka, hören Sie, so wahr ein Gott im
   Heaven's throne,   Himmel ist,
as truly you have nothing to forgive me.   so haben Sie mir nichts hier zu verzeihen!
If someone asks forgiveness, it's for you to   Viel eher muss ich Ihnen, wenn ich kann,
   ask it,   verzeihen,
for telling me what you have told me, and   was Sie zu mir geredet haben und in
   in such a tone!   welchem Ton!

MANDRYKA
(staring at Matteo, grimly)

You want a blind man, but my eyes are all [28] Ich müsste blind sein, und hab' leider
   too seeing!   scharfe Augen,
You want a deaf man, but I'm very keen of   ich müsste taub sein, und hab' leider gute
   hearing!   Ohren,
You want a man who is weak of mind. [26] ich müsste schwach im Kopfe sein — dann
   Such a man   vielleicht,

might be stupid enough to see but not recognise him,	dass ich das Invididuum nicht erkennen täte
nor understand what kind of a game you're playing in the night!	[15] und nicht verstünde, was hier für ein Spiel gespielt wird bei der Nacht.

MATTEO
(incensed by the insults he reads in Mandryka's eyes and expression)

Enough! If by chance you have any rights here, any titles,	Mein Herr, wenn Sie hier irgendwelche Rechte
even though they're very new, I'm at your disposal!	besitzen, wenn auch erst seit kurzer Zeit — ich stehe zur Verfügung!

ARABELLA
(between the two)

Yes, he is entitled. He has *all* the rights! For I have vowed [21, 6, 18]	Ja, alle Rechte besitzt dieser Herr, denn er ist mein
to love him. But you don't have any rights over me, no right whatsoever! [13, 10]	Verlobter, und Sie besitzen das Leiseste nicht, auch nicht einen Schatten von Rechten!
You know that, why don't you say so?	Sagen Sie selber!

MATTEO
(hesitatingly, tormented)

I've . . . no right . . . [10a]	Nein . . . keines . . .

ARABELLA
(to Mandryka)

You heard him!	Sie hören!

MANDRYKA

If only you'd let him finish his sentence.[10, 5]	Hätten Sie den Herrn ausreden lassen!
A little word had remained on his tongue still —	Ein kleines Wort war ihm noch auf der Zunge.
'I've . . . no right . . . only' . . . I could almost hear it,	'Nein, keines — ausser' hat er sagen wollen
but then he swallowed it. [28]	und hat es schnell verschluckt!
I saw it, that silent little word, I saw his lips move.	Ich aber, ich hab' es noch gesehn auf seinen Lippen.

ARABELLA [10a, 27]

Matteo, I have never known you for a cad!	Matteo, nie hab' ich für niedrig Sie gekannt!
What do you try to do?	Was tun Sie jetzt an mir —!
To vent a childish spite, before the world would you disgrace me?	Sie wollen mich aus Trotz vor aller Welt kompromittieren!
You have made up your mind to wreck my marriage!	Sie wollen meine Heirat mir verderben!

ADELAIDE

The miserable cheat! He thinks he can force us to give him our daughter!	Unsel'ger Intrigant! So will er die Hand meines Kindes erschleichen!

MANDRYKA
(taking one step closer to Matteo)

'Only . . .'. Don't try to hide the truth in silence! [6]	'Ausser —' Heraus mit der verschwiegenen Wahrheit!

MATTEO
(firmly)

No word! No word!	Kein Wort! Kein Wort!

MANDRYKA [15, 7, 8]
(to Arabella)

'Only the right . . .', that's what he wanted to tell you —	Ausser den Rechten, hat er sagen wollen,
'Only the right which this night bestows'!	die diese Nacht verliehen hat!

Do try again! Between the two of you alone
he might not mind to speak about it.

Versuchen Sie, vielleicht zu Ihnen ganz allein
[5, 6] wird er ein Wörterl drüber sagen!

ARABELLA
(*to Matteo*)

Is there anything
at all that you still want to tell me?

Haben Sie
vor diesem Herrn mir noch etwas zu sagen?

MATTEO
(*shaking his head*)

No!

Nein!

MANDRYKA

Let me congratulate you sincerely,
on so much luck with beautiful women —
and also on your tact.
I wonder which is greater.

[14] Ich gratuliere Ihnen, Herr Leutnant,
zu Ihrem Glück bei schönen Frauen und
[15] Ihrer Diskretion,
die beiden sind gleich gross.

ARABELLA
(*to Waldner*)

You've heard what he has said?

[28] Hast du gehört, Papa?

WALDNER

Mandryka, you'll give me satisfaction for
this outrage!
My dear, where are my pistols? What? I've
sold them? What a shame!
I shall find means to get a pair of pistols.

Mandryka, dafür wirst du Genugtuung
mir geben!
Wo sind meine Pistolen? Was — verkauft?
O Sakrament!
Ich werd' mir andere zu verschaffen wissen.

ARABELLA
(*standing motionless where she is, with a deeply agonised expression*)

I care no longer what may come. How
futile is this life!
What meaning is there in this world if such
a man can weaken,
if he cannot find the strength to trust me,
if he deserts me for a shadow's ghost!

Mag alles gehen, wie es will, das Leben ist
nichts wert!
Was ist an allem in der Welt, wenn dieser
Mann
[7, 5] so schwach ist und die Kraft nicht hat, an
mich zu glauben!
[20] Und mich dahingibt wegen eines Nichts!

HOTEL GUESTS
(*appearing upstairs*)

Do you know what's what? Who has been
caught with whom?
What? Someone ran away? With a
lieutenant?

Wie? Kennen Sie sich aus? Welcher hat
wen erwischt?
Was? Sie hat fortgewollt? Wie, mit dem
Leutnant?

ADELAIDE
(*with a large gesture to Waldner*)

No, surely this young man does not
deserve
that you honour him with a duel, Theodor!
Don't you see that this is an abject intrigue
of a twice-rejected suitor? That is obvious!

[6] Nein, dieser junge Mensch ist es nicht
wert,
[13] vor deine Pistole zu kommen, Theodor!
[15] Das ist die niederträcht'ge Kabale
des abgewiesenen Freiers und nichts weiter!

WALDNER

Who's talking of Matteo? It's Mandryka
From whom I must have satisfaction!

Von dem da redet niemand. Der
Mandryka —
[28, 6] der ist mir Genugtuung schuldig!

MATTEO

I am the only guilty one. I'm taking back
the words I spoke,

[10] Ich bin allein der Schuldige. Ich nehme
jedes Wort zurück,

101

and every glance. You must have mis- [6, 12] und jeden Blick! Missdeutet hat man alles,
understood me:
I did not mean a single word of those that ich habe nichts von dem gemeint, was Sie
you imagined. zu hören glaubten.
If anyone is to be blamed, it is I! Wenn jemand Strafe hier verdient, so bin
ich's.

WALDNER
(sharply)

Smear her first, and then again, suddenly, Eintunken und reinwaschen wiederum in
you try a white-wash — einem Atem,
that's not the way a gentleman behaved in das war zu meiner Zeit nicht Brauch bei
my time! Offizieren!

MANDRYKA
(addressing Arabella only)

The young lieutenant behaved as well as he Der junge Mensch benimmt sich brav wie
could have. [28, 6] möglich.
I think the time has come for you to pay Es wäre an der Zeit, dass Sie auf ihn
some heed
to him, and to *his* feelings, lovely child! [5] ein biss'l Rücksicht nehmen täten, schönes
Kind.
Confess the truth and own up just to me: Gestehn Sie mir die Wahrheit, mir allein!
he is your lover! I'll do my best to help, Es ist Ihr Liebhaber! Ich werde alles tun —
you can rely on me entirely, Arabella! Sie können sich auf mich verlassen,
Arabella!

ARABELLA
(looking firmly at him)

I swear by all that's holy to me, Mandryka, [7, 25] Bei meiner Seel' und Seligkeit, Mandryka,
the truth is on my side! die Wahrheit ist bei mir!

MANDRYKA

Please do not swear away your soul's [24] Nicht deine Seele so verschwören, Mädel!
salvation!
Deep in my heart, I ache for you! Mir tut das Herz so weh um dich!
(to himself)
Oh, Lord, what have I done that you bring O Gott, was tust du mir für eine Schande
shame on me through such a girl! an durch dieses Weib!
(again to Arabella, softly)
You can't deny it: I have seen the boy [10a] Wenn ich den Buben doch gesehn hab',
as he was giving him — I saw it clearly — wie er den Schlüssel ihm hat übergeben
the key to your room. [27] zu Ihrem Zimmer.

ARABELLA

I don't understand you. Was für einen Buben?

MANDRYKA

You know the one I mean; he is your Den Buben, Ihren Groom, den Sie
groom. geschickt!

ARABELLA

Not Zdenko? Good God! But who else? Den Zdenko? Mein Gott! Oder wen?

MANDRYKA [12, 18]

Aha! I want you to confess it, just to me. Aha! Ich will, dass Sie gestehn! Mir allein!

ARABELLA
(to herself)

It seems that hell itself must be against me! [7] Ist denn die Hölle gegen mich verschworen!

MANDRYKA

Am I to spare this man, who has destroyed Soll ich den Menschen dort, der mir mein
all my life's hopes — [6, 8] Leben ruiniert hat,
am I to spare him because he is your soll ich ihn schonen als Ihren Geliebten?
lover? Tell me that! Reden Sie!

ARABELLA [6, 13]

The truth is on my side, Mandryka, only truth is.
Everything else — that's clear to see — [10a, 6] speaks against me.

Die Wahrheit ist bei mir, Mandryka, nur die Wahrheit,
denn alles sonst — das seh' ich ja — ist gegen mich!

MANDRYKA

I ask you now, will you marry him, that [15, 7] Matteo
with whom you kept a secret lovers' rendezvous
a half hour after our engagement?!

Zum letzten Mal! Willst du heiraten dort den Menschen,
mit dem du hast das süsse Stelldichein gehabt
nach unsrer Verlobung zehn Minuten!

Dialogue.

ARABELLA
(*walking away from him*)

I have nothing to reply to your questions, Herr von Mandryka.

Ich habe nichts zu antworten, Herr von Mandryka, auf Ihre Fragen.

MANDRYKA
(*grimly*)

All right!
Go, hurry up and find an armourer, Welko —
whatever it may cost — I need some sabres —
two heavy sabres, with a cutting point.
Bring them at once, and make a doctor get up from his bed.
That's all we need. We'll use the winter-garden.

Auch gut.
Aufsperren lass dir eine Waffenhandlung, Welko,
soll kosten was es will, ich brauche Säbel!
Zwei schwere Säbel, scharfgeschliffene!
Sofort hierher! Und einen Doktor lass aufwecken,
sonst brauch' ich nichts. Dort ist der Wintergarten.

(*half-turning to Matteo*)

This is between the two of us. We do not need a witness.

Wir werden ohne Zeugen alles schon zu Ende bringen.

He takes his cigar case out of his pocket, thinks it over, offers one to Matteo who refuses, and lights one himself.

Would you, ladies and gentlemen, permit us to be alone till it is time?

Die Herrschaften vielleicht gestatten uns, allein zu bleiben bis dahin.

ZDENKA
(*calling from upstairs*)

Papa! Mama!

Papa! Mama!

Everyone looks up. Zdenka comes running down the stairs in a negligée, with her hair down, and kneels before her father. [The music resumes.] [6, 10a]

Papa!

Papa!

ADELAIDE
(*covering Zdenka with her cape*)

Zdenka! What is this get-up? It's dis- [12] graceful!

Zdenka! Was für ein Aufzug! Welche Schande!

ARABELLA [5, 15]

What is it dear? Zdenkerl, speak! I am with you.

Was ist geschehen! Zdenkerl! Red! Ich bin bei dir.

ZDENKA

One last adieu, then I will leave you. I must go!
I'll rest deep in the river, long before the day breaks.

Nur schnell adieu sag' ich euch allen.
Ich muss fort.
Ich muss ja in die Donau, noch bevor es Tag wird.

WALDNER

What are you saying?

Was soll das heissen?

103

HOTEL GUESTS
(murmuring)

Who is this girl? She's young, and very pretty!

Wer ist nun wieder dieses hübsches Mädel?

MANDRYKA
(to himself)

I recognise this face — I've seen it once before.

Ich hab' doch das Gesicht schon heute wo gesehn!

ZDENKA

Forgive me, all of you, and let me go.

Verzeiht mir alles nur — und lasst's mich fort!

I'm so ashamed — I die of shame. So let me go!

Ich schäm mich so — ich sterb' vor Scham — so lasst's mich fort!

The river be my grave, when the sun rises, [28] soon . . .

Vor Sonnenaufgang schon muss ich drin liegen tief —

after that you'll forgive me, every one of you, even Papa.

nachher dann werden alle mir verzeihn, auch der Papa!

ARABELLA
(embracing Zdenka)

You stay with me, and nothing that has happened, dear —

Du bleibst bei mir. Und was dir auch geschehen ist,

I don't care what it was — ever can alter our love for Zdenka!

an dir ist nichts geschehen, dass man dich weniger lieb müsst haben!

ZDENKA
(pointing at Matteo)

It was not his fault, for he never knew, and I alone . . .

Er ist unschuldig. Er hat nichts gewusst. Nur ich allein —

ADELAIDE

Still, poor, unhappy child!
Still, like the grave!

[3] Schweig, unglückseliges Kind!
Schweig bis uns Grab!

WALDNER

Be still yourself, and let her tell her story!

Schweig du sofort und reden lass das Mädel!

You see now what you get for all your masquerading!

Da habt ihr euren Lohn für eure Maskeraden.

ZDENKA
(to Arabella)

To you I'll tell my secret, only you alone.

Nur dir kann ich es sagen, dir nur, dir allein!

ARABELLA

I am with you, I'll never let you go. I am with you!

Ich bin bei dir, ich lass dich nicht im Stich, ich bin bei dir!

ZDENKA
(close by her)

He was convinced . . . that it was you! I [6, 15] was afraid —

Er hat geglaubt, dass du es bist! Ich hab's getan

afraid for him, Bella. You understand?

aus Angst um ihn, Bella, verstehst du mich?

Still now he does not know that it was I! [12]

Er weiss ja jetzt noch nicht, dass ich es war!

(full of fear)

Matteo!

Matteo!

MATTEO

What sweetest voice has called my name?

Welch süsse Stimme ruft mich an?

104

ZDENKA
(ashamed)

The voice of one who played you false, Matteo.	Die Stimme der Betrügerin, Matteo!
Your friend, your dear friend, your Zdenko speaks to you.	Dein Freund, dein einz'ger, dein Zdenko steht vor dir!
But I am Zdenka! Yes, I am Arabella's sister!	Ich bin ein Mädel, ach, ich war ja nie was andres!

MATTEO

My dearest friend, my lovely Zdenka . . . sweetest angel, you!	O du mein Freund! Du meine Freundin! Süsser Engel du!

ZDENKA

I ask you both for your forgiveness, you and her.	Dich muss ich um Verzeihung bitten, dich und sie,
Oh, my God!	euch beide — o mein Gott!

She covers her face with her hands.

ARABELLA

If love, because it is too great, must beg forgiveness, [5, 15, 6, 28]	Wenn zuviel Liebe um Verzeihung bitten muss,
then you must beg him to forgive you.	dann bitte ihn halt um Verzeihung!

She draws her close and kisses her.

MATTEO

The room was in darkness, and I never . . . never heard your voice.	Im Zimmer war's zu finster, deine Stimme hab' ich nicht gehört —
And yet I feel, as though from the beginning, [13, 5] I'd sensed the truth. My loving, tender Zdenka!	und doch ist mir, als hätt' ich es geahnt von Anfang an, o süsser kleiner Zdenko!

Zdenka looks at Matteo tenderly, but stays in Arabella's arms.

MANDRYKA [6, 18, 12, 10]
(to himself)

She is the boy I saw! I wish the ground would open!	Das Mädel war der Groom! Ich möcht' in Boden sinken!
How can I ever hope she will forgive me?	Wie soll sie jemals mir verzeihen können
How can I ever dare forgive myself?	wo ich mir selber nicht verzeihen kann!

Welko enters carrying two sabres. Behind him comes Djura, with two pistols in a box, and behind him a doctor. Mandryka sees them but motions them away.

WALDNER
has also seen them. With the cold determination of the gambler:

That's good! Now I have the opponent whom I want!	[23] Sehr gut. Jetzt habe ich mein richtiges Vis-à-vis.
This is a father's task — it's up to me.	Die Sache geht allein den Vater an.

THE THREE GAMBLERS

Oho! Oho!	Oho! Oho!

MANDRYKA
(paying no attention to Waldner, addressing himself to Arabella only) [8, 24, 5]

How can I stand before you, Arabella?	Wie steh' ich vor Ihnen, Arabella!
I know I don't deserve one single glance from you in all my life.	[18] Ich weiss, nicht einen Blick von Ihnen bin ich wert mein Lebenlang!
A clumsy peasant, with these sturdy fists I have, I thought I could . . .	[17] So wie ein Tölpel mit den beiden Fäusten da,
I thought a man could reach for happiness like that!	hab' ich gemeint, man dürfte greifen nach dem allergrössten Glück,
I am no longer worthy; I lost everything.	und bin unwert geworden — so im Handumdrehn,

105

Regret is all that's left me now — regret [6] und jetzt bleibt Reue und mich schämen
and shame until I die.   bis an meinen letzten Tag.

ARABELLA

Zdenkerl, you're so much kinder than I   [17] Zdenkerl, du bist die Bess're von uns
am.   zweien.
You have a heart more loving than mine,   Du hast das liebevollere Herz, und nichts
and nothing counts for you,   ist da für dich,
nothing in this world but what your heart [7] nichts in der Welt, als was dein Herz dich
may bid you do.   heisst zu tun.
I thank you, dear, you've given me a   [15] Ich dank dir schön, du gibst mir eine gute
golden lesson: Lehre,
it's not for us to want things, to demand   dass wir nichts wollen dürfen, nichts
them —   verlangen,
we must not weigh, we must not trade, nor[10a]abwägen nicht und markten nicht und
ever stint,   geizen nicht,
but give and love till the day we die.   nur geben und liebhaben immerfort!

She does not give Mandryka the one glance he is longing for, which would set everything right.

ZDENKA
(together with Arabella)

Your voice is soft and mild, you do not   Wie sanft du zu mir sprichst! Du bist nicht
bear a grudge.   bös auf mich!
You are kind, more than words can say. I   Du bist so unaussprechlich gut, ich kenn'
know you, no-one knows you like me, [5, 15, 17] dich, wie dich keiner kennt,
and all I do is always done out of love for   und immer möcht' ich alles dir zuliebe
you.   tun —
(alone)
I hoped to steal away, and to vanish,   und nur verschwinden hätt' ich mögen still
so that none of you would be hurt, but you   und euch nicht kränken! Aber du verstehst
understand me, you,   mich, du,
and you will not desert me whatever now   und wirst mich nicht verlassen, was auch
may come!   jetzt noch kommt!

MANDRYKA
(to himself, very faint-heartedly)

What now may come...   Was jetzt noch kommt —

ADELAIDE

O God! Oh, shame beyond all measure! [6, 5] O Gott! O Übermass der Schande!
Oh, how I wish this evening had not   O wäre dieser Abend nie gewesen!
happened!
I'm sure no fortune-teller told me such a   Das hat keine Prophetin mir vorausgesagt!
thing!

WALDNER [23, 24, 8, 28]
(firmly)

What's now to come? That's very clear!   Was jetzt noch kommt, das ist ganz klar!

He makes a determined move, with a glance at the pistols.

ARABELLA
(to Zdenka)

But, come what may, I am with you.   Was immer kommt, ich bin bei dir!

MANDRYKA
(his eyes on Arabella, in a strained voice)

What now may come...   Was jetzt noch kommt —

ZDENKA
(fearful)

Papa!   Papa!

MATTEO

Angel from Heaven!   [15]   Engel vom Himmel,

106

God will guard you, he will not let the world defile you!

da sei Gott vor, dass dich die Welt beschmutzen dürfte!

MANDRYKA
(still in a choked voice)

What now may come ...

Was jetzt noch kommt —

He turns as though going away.

ARABELLA [5, 25]
(softly, over Zdenka's shoulder.)

Mandryka!

Mandryka!

She gives him her hands.

MANDRYKA [7, 25]
(bending over Arabella's hand.)

I am not worthy of your forgiveness.

Ich bin nicht wert solcher Verzeihung!

ARABELLA

Still, Mandryka.
We will say nothing more. It seems

we have forgotten what it was that happened here.
It was no fault of ours.
Good will is now the bond that shall unite us,
for all that still may come.

Still, Mandryka!
[20] Wir sprechen jetzt nichts mehr. Wir haben jetzt
vergessen, was uns hier geschehen ist!
Es war nicht unsre Schuld.
Wir wollen alle guten Willen haben,
für das, was jetzt noch kommt!

MANDRYKA

For all that still may come?
With a quick decision he takes Matteo by the hand and leads him over to Waldner.
Let's post the banns!
With this lieutenant I appear before you, noble Captain and Count.
I bow to you. I ask in his name — he is my [18] friend —
that you will not deny to him the hand of [15] this young lady.

Für das, was jetzt noch kommt?

Brautwerbung kommt!
Mit diesem Herrn da trete ich vor Ihnen, hochgeborener Herr,
verneige mich und bitte für ihn als meinen Freund,
dass Sie die Hand nicht weigern ihm von diesem jungen Fräulein.

Waldner makes a gesture indicating 'no'.

Do not deny what ardent love has bestowed on him!

Nicht weigern ihm, was grosse Liebe ihm verliehen hat!

ZDENKA
(weakly)

Matteo! Papa! What is the meaning?
I need not leave?

[10a] Matteo! Papa! Was ist das alles?
Muss ich nicht fort?

ARABELLA

You must be happy now, as you deserve!

Du musst jetzt glücklich sein, wie du's verdienst!

Waldner is moved and kisses Arabella.

WALDNER
(to Zdenka)

Don't cry, my darling. And you, young man, let me shake your hand.

[17] So wein' nicht, Kleine. Reichen Sie mir Ihre Hand, mein Herr.

He shakes Matteo's hand.

ADELAIDE

O Theodor! What a reversal!

O Theodor, welch eine Wendung!

WALDNER

Colossal!   Kolossal!

ADELAIDE
(*in tears*)

O Theodor!   O Theodor!

Waldner embraces Adelaide casually, and immediately turns to his fellow gamblers.

WALDNER

I am at your disposal. Let us go!   [1] Ich stehe zur Verfügung, meine Herren!

He rushes off, the gamblers behind him.

HOTEL GUESTS
(*muttering*)

We might as well sleep. This is the end of it.   Wir gehen schlafen. Jetzt passiert nichts mehr!

They all retire to their rooms.

ARABELLA

Take her upstairs, Mama.   [7, 15] Führ sie hinauf, Mama!

Mandryko takes a step towards Arabella.

Now let us say no more.   [25, 7] Wir sprechen jetzt nicht mehr,
We'll wait until the sun shines. Don't you think so too?   bis wieder heller Tag ist! Meinen Sie nicht auch?

Adelaide and Zdenka climb the stairs to the first floor.

ZDENKA [12]
(*tenderly*)

Matteo!   Matteo!

ARABELLA

Come on! Tomorrow is near, then he'll be yours for ever.   [15, 6] Geh nur, er kommt morgen früh, dann hast du ihn für immer.

Matteo leaves. Mandryko is anxious and tense; Arabella addresses him casually:

Could your servant go to the court outside and, from the well bring me a glass of water to my room?   Kann Ihr Diener im Hof zum Brunnen gehn [15] und mir ein Glas recht frisches Wasser bringen dort hinauf?

Welko rushes off.

I think that it might do me good. We did a lot of talking.   Ich glaub', es täte mir ganz gut nach dieser [20, 15, 12] Unterhaltung.

She goes upstairs. Mandryka looks after her until she has disappeared. Someone must have turned out one more lamp; it is much darker.

MANDRYKA [28, 7, 22]

She has no glance for me, she does not say goodnight,   [24] Sie gibt mir keinen Blick, sie sagt nicht gute Nacht,
She leaves me here, and goes. But then, what else did I deserve?   [13] Sie lässt mich stehn und geht. Hab' ich was anderes verdient?
What is deserved in all this world? Deserved . . . for what?   Was ist verdient auf dieser Welt? Verdient ist nichts.
A beating is deserved for such a lout as me!   Stockprügel sind verdient für einen Kerl wie mich —

Yet, as a gift, I'd have gladly taken one of her glances —   [5] aber geschenkt hätt' ich gerne einen Blick genommen —
or even half a glance!   so einen halben Blick!

Welko comes back with a glass on a tray, and looks at Mandryka questioningly.

Take it upstairs.   Geh nur hinauf!

Welko goes upstairs.

She meant nothing at all, only a glass of water,   Sie hat gar nichts gemeint, als ein Glas Wasser haben
and then, no longer sees me! Or perhaps she meant to mock me!   und Ruh vor meinem Anblick. Oder spotten hat sie wollen.

| Perhaps . . . But if she mocks me, that alone is a blessing she grants me, and an undeserved one, God knows that! | Vielleicht—? Wenn sie nur spottet, wenigstens ist's doch schon eine Gnade, eine unverdiente, das weiss Gott! |

Arabella appears upstairs and glances down to see whether Mandryka is still there. Her face lights up. She takes the glass and walks down the stairs, Welko behind her. Mandryka turns around and sees Arabella with the glass, as she is walking down the stairs slowly and solemnly. In his sudden joy he takes a few steps back. [24, 15, 7, 20]

Josephine Barstow as Arabella at ENO, 1984 (photo: Clive Barda)

ARABELLA
(on the last step)

I'm very glad, Mandryka, that you have stayed and have not gone away.
This glass here I intended to empty all alone,
and while I'm drinking forget the evil that has been today . . .
and then, to go to bed and no longer think of you and me,
until a radiant day once more were shining over us.
But later, when I felt that you were standing in the dark,
I knew a higher might had touched my heart,
and touched it to the core.
So I need not refresh myself with any drink.
No, I'm refreshed because I feel that love is mine,
and thus this drink that none has touched I offer to my friend —
this evening, when I'm parting from the girl that I have been.

Das war sehr gut, Mandryka, dass Sie noch nicht fortgegangen sind —
[25] das Glas da hab' ich austrinken wollen ganz allein
auf das Vergessen von dem Bösen, was gewesen ist,
und still zu Bette gehn und nicht denken mehr an Sie und mich,
[17] bis wieder heller Tag gekommen wäre über uns.
[7] Dann aber, wie ich Sie gespürt hab' hier im Finstern stehn,
hat eine grosse Macht mich angerührt
von oben bis ans Herz,
dass ich mich nicht erfrischen muss mit einem Trunk:
nein, mich erfrischt schon das Gefühl von meinem Glück
[26] und diesen unberührten Trunk kredenz' ich meinem Freund
den Abend, wo die Mädchenzeit zu Ende ist für mich.

She steps down and hands him the glass. Welko takes the empty tray out of Arabella's hand and leaves. Mandryka empties the glass quickly and holds it high in his right hand.

MANDRYKA

As true as from this glass no-one shall ever drink again!
Thus you are mine, and yours am I, for time without end!

[25] So wahr aus diesem Glas da keiner trinken wird nach mir,
so bist du mein und ich bin dein auf ewige
[17] Zeit!

He smashes the glass against the steps.

ARABELLA
She stands on the step again, and places her hand on his shoulder.

And so we are betrothed as lovers evermore;
In grief, in joy, to hurt and to forgive!

[7] Und so sind wir Verlobte und Verbundene auf Leid und Freud und Wehtun und Verzeihn!

MANDRYKA

Forever you, my angel, and to all that yet may come to us!

Auf immer, du mein Engel, und auf alles, was da kommen wird!

ARABELLA

You will believe me?

[10a] Und du wirst glauben—?

MANDRYKA

And you'll always be as you are?

Und du wirst bleiben, wie du bist?

ARABELLA

I cannot be another — take me as I am.

[17] Ich kann nicht anders werden, nimm mich, wie ich bin!

She falls into his arms. He kisses her. She tears herself away and runs upstairs. Mandryka stands looking after her.

Curtain.

Selective discography *by Cathy Peterson*

Conductor Orchestra/Opera House Date	*L. Mataĉic* **Philharmonia** 1954	*G. Solti* **Vienna PO** 1957	*W. Sawallisch* **Bavarian State Opera** 1981
Arabella	E. Schwarzkopf	L. della Casa	J. Varady
Zdenka	A. Felbermayer	H. Gueden	H. Donath
Mandryka	J. Metternich	G. London	D. Fischer-Dieskau
Waldner	T. Schlott	O. Edelmann	W. Berry
Matteo	N. Gedda	A. Dermota	A. Dallapozza
Adelaide	—	I. Malaniuk	H. Schmidt
Elemer	M. Dickie	W. Kmentt	H. Winkler
UK disc number	RLS 751	GOS 571/3	SLS 5224
US disc number	Angel 35194	GOS 571/3	DSCX 3917
	(highlights only)		

The Sawallisch recording of *Arabella* is outstanding for both its artistic and sonic qualities. Lisa della Casa's fine portrayal of the title role makes the Solti version well worth hearing.

For a detailed analysis of the history of *Arabella* on records, readers are referred to Michael Kennedy's article in *Opera on Record 3* (ed. Alan Blyth, Hutchinson, 1984).

Bibliography

There are two major biographical English studies of Strauss: Norman del Mar's *Richard Strauss: A critical commentary on his life and works* (London, 3 volumes, 1962-1972; 1978) and William Mann's *Richard Strauss: A Critical Study of the Operas* (London, 1964). Michael Kennedy's volume on the composer in the Master Musician series (London, 1976) is the best short introduction. The long and absorbing correspondence between Strauss and Hofmannsthal (Cambridge, 1981) is of exceptional interest. Among the many books on Austria during the last decades of the Habsburg rule are the superb photographic survey by Franz Hubmann, *The Habsburg Empire*, ed. Andrew Wheatcroft (Verlag Fritz Molden, 1971) and Martin Esslin's book on *Freud, The Man, His World, His Influence* (London, 1900). Michael Hamburger's excellent translations of Hofmannsthal (including *Lucidor* and *Arabella*) are available in *Poems and Verse Plays* (London, 1961) and *Selected Plays and Libretti* (London, 1964), and his *Hofmannsthal: Three Essays* (Princeton, Bollingen Series, 1961, 1963, 1972) sets the libretto in the context of the poet's other work.

William Mann's *Musical Synopsis* is an extract from his book mentioned above, which is shortly to be republished by Cambridge University Press.

Contributors

Michael Ratcliffe, a former Literary Editor and Chief Book Reviewer of *The Times*, is now Theatre Critic of *The Observer* and is working on a biography of Goethe.

William Mann, formerly Chief Music Critic of *The Times* (1960-1982) is currently Artistic Director of the 1985 Bath Festival. He is the author of studies of the operas of Mozart and Strauss, and a history book called *Music in Time*.

Patrick Smith is the author of *The Tenth Muse, a Historical Study of the Opera Libretto* and *A Year at the Met.*. He is New York music correspondent for *The Times* and *Opera* magazine and is Book Editor of *Musical America*.

Karen Forsyth was McIlrath Junior Research Fellow at St Hilda's College, Oxford from 1979-82. She is the author of *'Ariadne auf Naxos' by Richard Strauss and Hugo von Hofmannsthal* and has writen an article on 'Stefan Zweig's adaptations of Ben Jonson' as well as other, shorter pieces on the Strauss/Hofmannsthal collaboration.